INDIA AND CHINA

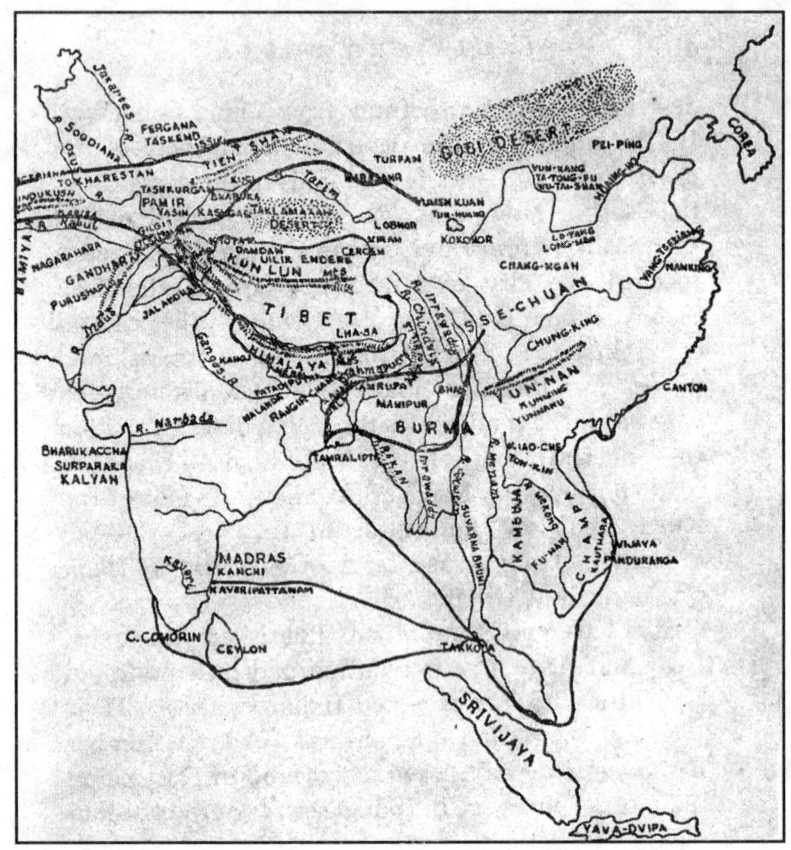

Routes to China

INDIA AND CHINA

A Study of Cultural Relations

K.M. Panikkar

First Published 1957
First LG Edition 2016
Reprinted 2025

ISBN 978-93-83723-14-0

Published by
LG PUBLISHERS DISTRIBUTORS
49, Gali No. 14, Pratap Nagar
Mayur Vihar Phase I, Delhi 110 091
Tel: 011 2279 5641 email: lgpdist@gmail.com

Leser Typeset at
Arpit Printographers, Delhi-92

Printed in India at
D.K. Fine Art Press (P) Ltd.

Contents

Introduction

Early this year, the Vice-Chancellor of the Maharaja Sayaji Rao University of Baroda honoured me by an invitation to deliver three lectures on India and China. The lectures were in commemoration of the late Maharaja Sayaji Rao, one of the fathers of Indian nationalism and a truly great and far-sighted prince whom I had the privilege of knowing for over twenty years. Of his foresight and patriotism, the following conversation, recorded by His Highness the Aga Khan in his recent book of memories, should be sufficient evidence. Speaking to His Highness the Aga Khan in 1907—forty years before India achieved independence—the Maharaja said that when India became free the first thing that the leaders would have to do would be to get rid of the princely states: for, in his opinion, there could be no unity so long as the princes remained as rulers of semi-independent states. Himself an ornament of the princely order, he was wise enough to realize that there was no place for a feudal system in modern times and that Indian unity was too precious a thing to be sacrificed for petty dynastic or personal interests. That a university established in free republican India is named after him shows how greatly India honours the name of this great patriot.

In inviting me to lecture on India and China, the University authorities perhaps expected me to deal with the political relations which have developed in recent times between the two countries. Those relations are undoubtedly important. They represent a major fact in the history of Asia today. But it would not have been possible to develop such a relationship, even on the basis of *Pancha Shila,* but for the historic background of a thousand years and more of close association between the peoples of India and China. There is some idea, not only among the Western scholars but even among our own people, that the past relations between India and China were a question of a few pilgrims coming to India and some monks going from here to China. In fact, one of our most distinguished elder statesmen enquired of me, after reading Rene Grousset's remarkable book dealing with the travels in India of Yuan Chuan entitled *In the Footsteps of the Buddha,* whether there were no Indian scholars who had similarly travelled in China and whether anything was known about them. This enquiry brought home to me the fact that very few people in India knew anything about India's past relations with China.

And yet, the thousand years of contact between India and China constitute one of the central facts of Asian history. It is this prolonged contact which has been the major factor in the shaping of the Asian mind, for, from China, its influence radiated to Korea, Japan, Mongolia and other more distant lands. Okakura, the famous Japanese thinker, writing in 1922, declared:

> The classic civilizations of China and India shine the brighter by contrast with the night that has overtaken them.... The children of the Hoang Ho and the Ganges had from early days evolved a culture comparable with the era of the highest enlightenment in Greece and Rome, one which even foreshadowed the trend of advanced thought in modern Europe. Buddhism, introduced into China and the farthest East during the early centuries of the Christian era, bound together the Vedic and Confucian ideals in a single web and brought about the unification of Asia. A vast system of intercourse flowed throughout the extent of the Buddha land. Tidings of any fresh philosophical achievement in the university of

> Nalanda or in the monasteries of Kashmir were brought by pilgrims and wandering monks to the thought centres of China, Korea, and Japan..... Peace married art to art. From this synthesis of the whole of Asian life a fresh impetus was given to each nation.... It was a terrible blow to Buddha land [i.e. to the unity of Asian culture] when Islam interposed a barrier between China and India greater than the Himalayas themselves. (Okakura, *Ideals of the East.*)

Undoubtedly, what gave a spiritual and cultural unity to non-Islamic Asia was this prolonged contact between India and China. It is, in spite of nearly a thousand years of interruption, still a major strand in Asian history. The Sinic and Indic worlds, firm in their own civilizations, remain the two germinal centres of Asian life, but if, in spite of many differences, these two civilizations have many things in common, it is the result of the thousand years of contact between the two peoples.

The Indian and Chinese civilizations confronted each other in the Valleys of the Mekong and the Menang to create a civilization which has endured to our day and is showing signs of a vigorous revival. The states of Southeast Asia, by and large, represent the spirit of that synthesis. The deserts and the Steppes of Central Asia and the mighty tableland of Tibet prevented such a direct confrontation on the northern and the north-eastern side. But it was in this area that the exchange of culture was most vigorous. Here, it was not a confrontation, but and exchange, for the peoples of the intervening area, because of their nomadic character and also for the reason that they were on the main routes of international trade, acted as the carriers of culture. The Indianized kingdoms of what Sir Aurel Stein has appropriately called Serindia, Uddiyana, Khotan and Kuchi, now known only from records and hardly mentioned in books of history, whose records and achievements were wiped out by conquerors, played a part in this great exchange of ideas which can hardly be over-estimated. They are the forgotten chapters of Asian history, chapters without an understanding of which many aspects of Indian and Chinese history must themselves remain obscure. One of the keys to the understanding of Asia, of the unity which people now recognize but cannot understand lies buried in the ruins and mounds of Turkestan.

In the present lectures I have attempted only to indicate the main lines of Sino-Indian relationships in the past. A detailed study must not merely include a history of the intermediate kingdoms of Central Asia, but also a fuller analysis of the kingdoms of Southeast Asia, Funan, Champa, Kamboj and Indonesia. It must also include the yet unexplored history of Tibet.

I have added as appendixes essays on the importance of Tibet in the later period of Sino-Indian relations, on Chinese pilgrims in India and on the interactions of India and China on art, though they were not a part of the lectures delivered at Baroda.

In conclusion I express my thanks to Srimati Hansa Mehta, the Vice-Chancellor of the Baroda University, for her invitation to deliver these lectures under the auspices of the University.

K.M.P.

I

In the heart of the Gobi Desert, near an oasis known as Yumen or the Jade Gate, which formed the limit of the old Chinese Empire, as its name indicates, there is a small well-watered valley, sheltered by hills on all sides, known all over the world now as Tunghuan. There, on the sides of the hills, are excavated hundreds of caves, beautified by mural paintings and sculptures of very high quality, depicting scenes from the life of the Buddha and from the Jataka stories. The Tunghuan caves, a veritable treasure-house of art, till the 11th century housed a great international monastery; for one of the striking features of the later paintings in the caves is the evidence of Turkish, Iranian and other influences, which mingle with the predominantly Sino-Indian character of Tunghuan art.

How did so large a monastery, with a vigorous artistic and cultural life and capable of accommodating thousands of monks and laymen, come into existence in the Gobi Desert, just outside the main gate of entry into the great Empire of China? It could certainly not have been the desire to meditate in the desert that led the monks to establish themselves in the walled-in, tiny oasis, to dig out, with infinite patience, its numerous caves and embellish them with paintings of supreme beauty, to carry on a vigorous life there for 700 years and then suddenly to disappear from history.

The fact is that Tunghuan was the last stage of the toilsome journey from India and the Indianized kingdoms of Central Asia to the great Empire of China. It was the last resting place, before entering China proper, of the scholars, missionaries and other travellers who were continuously arriving from India, Khotan, Kuchi and other areas of Buddhist civilization; as also the first stage for those undertaking the strenuous journey across the snows of the Pamirs, or the desert lands of Central Asia, to visit the holy places of Buddhism in India. At Tunghuan, the three northern routes from India met. It was the great clearing-house for all travellers to China from the north-west, and the monastery with its temples, caves for meditation and large collection of books provided an ideal resting place.

Between China and India lies 'a continent of plateaus' which culminate in the steppe of the Pamirs. To the east lie the Himalayas, with its immense plateau of Tibet. To the north are the only slightly less formidable mountain barriers, the Tien Shan and the Altai ranges. The great Gobi lies between the Altai range and the Tien Shan, with the Tarim basin at one end. The Kazak steppes separate the Tien Shan from the Altai. There we have a picture of the formidable geographical barriers between India and China, barriers consisting of high mountain ranges and vast steppes and deserts extending over hundreds of thousands of square miles. But the deserts and the steppes have never been great obstacles in the way of trade and movement. Caravan routes traversed them. Mountains can be avoided by following circuitous routes and by making use of passes. Thus the gap between the Tien Shan and the Altai Mountains called the Zungarian Gate provided a convenient opening. Of the three routes, the first lay through Afghanistan, with stages at Jalalabad, then known as Nagarahara, and at Bamiyan, where an immense monastery, the ruins of which can still be seen, provided the travellers with the necessary facilities. The work of French archaeologists in this region has shown us what a great centre of Indian culture Bamiyan was in the first millennium of the Christian era. From there, through Bactria, the area of Samarkand, the route went eastwards over the passes of the Tien Shan Mountains. A second route which was shorter but more difficult lay through Kashmir and Gilgit to Kashgar, and from there to Tokhau. A third was directly to Kashgar and from there along the Tarim basin to Tunghuan. Aurel Stein has traced the monasteries along this route which provided the halting places and other necessary facilities for travellers.

A distinguished writer, the late Puntambaker, describes the route to India from China as follows. In the middle of the desert of Gobi there is the desert of Hani. It is watered by streams from the Barkul Mountains, at the eastern end of the Tien Shan. From Hani, by camel and cart, caravans reached the city of Ku-Cheng, beyond the Tien Shan. From Ku-Cheng to Urmitzi, the capital of Sinkiang.... From Urmitzi the southern road passes over the Tien Shan to Tufan. From Tufan westward, the road passes through a desert, reaching the southern foot of the Tien Shan. Then the road continues to Kashgar.... along the foot of the Kuen Leun to the south, to the west through Yarkand. It branches off in the south to India via Yasin and Gilgit.

All along this route there flourished kingdoms, great and small, the population of which professed Buddhism and had accepted Indian culture. Their language was based on Sanskrit. A large number of manuscripts have been discovered in this region and most of them are in Indian scripts of the Kushan and Gupta periods. Some of the dynasties which ruled in these areas were also of Indian origin. Official documents in an Indian dialect have been recovered from the Khotan area. Kuchi was also a state of considerable importance. Its rulers who bore such significantly Hindu names as Hara Deva were champions of Indian culture. In fact, up to the very borders of China on its north-west side, kingdoms which had imbibed the spirit of Indian culture were in existence at least from the 1st century AD.

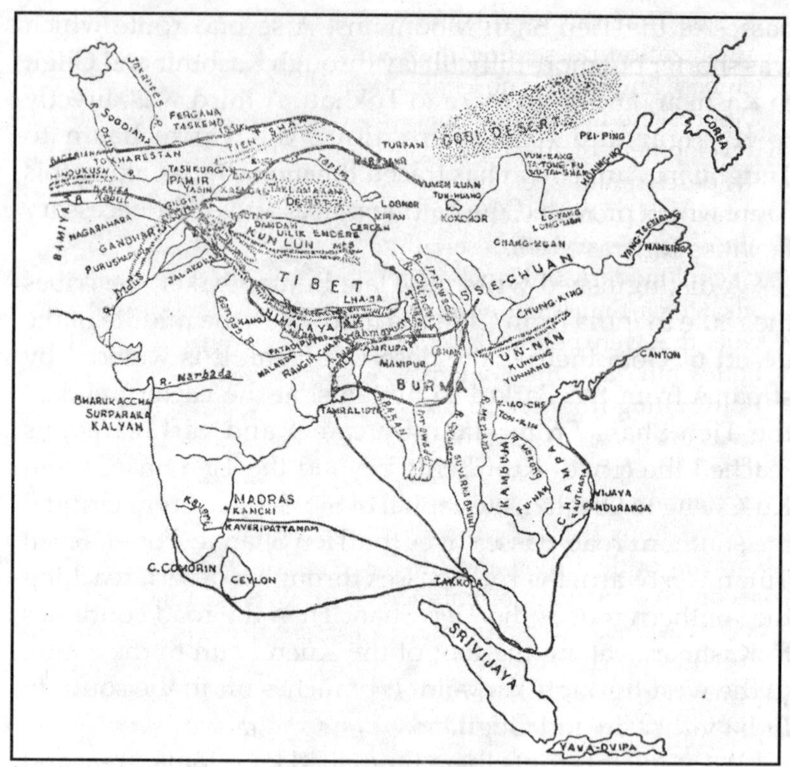

ROUTES TO CHINA

The role of the desert and the steppe as the carriers of civilization between India and China has been well described recently by an Italian scholar:

> India and China, with Iran at their borders, are the pivots on which turns the cultural dynamism of the Far East. But this constant conflict and exchange of ideas and forms of civilization took place for the most part on a ground where other political forces and other forms of life prevailed. The steppe belt to the north of China and India played a great part in the development of Asia as the medium through which all kinds of religious and artistic influences travelled, and as a political and military factor outrunning even the possibilities of the two major cultural powers. While it is true that the history of the civilization of the Far East hinges on China and India, while it

> is true that the world has never seen another political organization possessing the stability and continuity of the Chinese Empire, it is no less true that the steppes and the Gobi Desert were factors of prime importance in determining the development of Asian history. This holds good not only for the purely political element provided by the great, but usually ephemeral, nomad empires which arose at irregular intervals in the steppes and the desert. But the peaceful and rich caravan cities of modern Sinkiang, made wealthy by the active trade in silk which flourished on that route down to the 8th century, cities that were politically quiescent and objects of the greed of both China and the nomads, acted as essential agencies for transmitting from one to the other of the three great cultural areas the germs of reciprocal fertilization. And in this process they developed a composite and in some ways unique civilization of their own.
>
> Without the steppe, without its nomad states and its caravan trade, China and India would have been limited to secondary currents of contact through Southeast Asia. In Southeast Asia, as I have already mentioned, an immense work of civilization had been carried on for more than one thousand years; but it was this very work, arduous and difficult as it was, which led China and India to face each other there, since the earliest ages, as two opposite civilizations, each unchangeably firm in itself, with no possibility of fruitful exchanges. For Central Asia, on the contrary, I need only recall the part played by the caravan routes of the Tarim basin in the transmission eastward of Buddhism and its artistic elements, which so deeply affected, by action and reaction, the evolution of Chinese society.

When did this vital area of Central Asia come under the cultural influence of India? The area on this side of the Hindukush was a part of the Mauryan Empire, a separate viceroyalty with that ancient seat of learning, Taxila, as its capital. During the reign of the first three Mauryan emperors, and especially in the time of Asoka, who was a zealous cultural missionary, this area became the advance base of Indian life. The Yue-chis who established themselves in the succeeding era, became, under their adopted name of Kushans, the great carriers of Indian culture. The empire of Kanishka was, we should remember, a major factor in Central Asian history. It extended from the Gangetic Valley into the depths of Central Asia, including the Khotan region. Kanishka was an ardent Buddhist who convened an ecumenical council in Kashmir according to some, and in Gandhara according to others. The Central Asian territories seem to have definitely come under Indian influence during this period, the Kushana imperial government playing a notable part in its spread.

For nearly eight centuries (125 BC to AD 650) Bactriana was, in effect, occupied by the Kushans who also extended their sway to the entire valley of the Kabul. Connected politically with the Indo-Gangetic Valley and separated on the other hand from Iran proper by a desert, it fell gradually under Indian influence and the ancient religion of the Magi gave place to that of the Brahmins, and, later on, to that of the Buddhists. The Greek writers of the period always cite Bactriana with India and mention thousands of Brahmanas and Sramanas who reside there. In fact, the area was during this long period a great centre of Hindu-Buddhist culture.

The part played by these borderlands in the spread of Indian culture cannot be over-emphasized. It is in these areas, with their centres at Taxila, Kandahar and Kabul, that a new and dynamic Indian life developed with the full participation of the Sakas, Kushans, Bactrians and Parthians. They found in Mahayana Buddhism a rich and satisfying religion and the spread of this religion was accompanied by that of Indian languages and literature; arts and architecture, science, medicine and philosophy. From the 2nd century BC this area thus becomes an advance base of Indian life.

The Chinese annalists who have conserved for us precious data regarding these Scythian princes describe them as zealous Buddhists. By the middle of the 7th century, a major revolution took place in this important area. M. Chavannes, the famous French Sinologist, has established, on the basis of his analysis of Central Asian records, that in the first half of the 8th century, the Chinese had expanded into the great Central Asian basins, carrying their authority to the western side of the Pamirs. The Indo-Buddhist states thus passed under their authority, and the active rule of the Chinese reached Gilgit on the Indian border. The two civilizations met here.

The period, when Hindu-Buddhist civilization extended into Central Asia, was also one of great Chinese expansion. The 'silk road' to the West had been opened in the 2nd century BC. From a cemetery site in the Lop Desert in Chinese Turkestan, Sir Aurel Stein recovered some silk weavings of this date. In 188 BC the great Chinese envoy, Chang Chien, visited these areas and went up to the Yue-Chi capital. He stayed many years in those parts. In the capital of the Yue-Chi kingdom in the heart of Central Asia, which the Chinese were visiting for the first time, he came across goods from south-west China which, on enquiry, he was told were brought by Indian merchants across the plains of Hindustan. Clearly, long before the north-western route to China was opened, commercial communications had been fully developed between China and India, enabling Indian caravans to carry Chinese products into Central Asia. What was this important route which had connected the two countries long before the development of Khotan, Kuchi and other Central Asian states in the 2nd century BC? As the produce which Chang Chien saw came from south-west China, that route evidently was from Yunnan to the cities of Bengal, which, with Tamralipti as the great emporium and port, dominated the maritime trade of the period. Indian traders from the Gangetic Valley passed along the routes which, in our times, came to be organized during the Sino-Japanese war as the great Burma-China Road. Starting from the Gangetic Valley, running across Assam to Burma and then to Yunnan, this caravan route was frequented by Indian merchants from the earliest times. It is interesting to note that in the *Mahabharata* the 'Cheenas' are mentioned in company with the 'Pragjotishas', or the Assamese, reflecting thereby the association of China in the popular mind with the peoples in the neighbourhood of Assam. In fact, this connection between India's eastern districts and China persisted for long. At the time when Yuan Chuan (Hiouen Tsang) visited Kamarupa (7th century AD), the route was still being used. He noted: 'To the east of Kamarupa, the country is a series of hills and hillocks without any principal city and it reached to the south-west barbarians [aboriginal races] of China; hence the inhabitants are akin to the Man and the Lao.' Szechuan, it was reported to him, was two months journey from Kamarupa.

As Yuan Chuan also noted, many of the tribes of the Assam area bear a close resemblance to the people of south-west China. Anthropologists maintain that Kamakhya worship originated in the tribal areas of south China and the name of the goddess Kamakhya is itself said to be derived from Chinese. When Yuan Chuan visited the country he noticed that popular Chinese tunes had penetrated into the Brahmaputra Valley.

Another and, perhaps, easier route for commerce was along the coast to Arakan, and from there to Pagan and thence to Yunnan. The monastery sites along this route, which was less hazardous, have now been located and we can therefore assume that, at least during certain periods, the line of communication was also frequented by merchants and others.

The importance of these great routes which first brought China and India together, long before the Central Asian routes were opened consequent upon the Indianization of Central Asia in the 2nd century BC, was for long overlooked for two reasons. First, the Central Asian route, once opened, lay through highly civilized states which provided facilities such as rest-houses, monasteries, staging points, etc., while the eastern routes were dominated by mountains which 'were hard to pass' and where 'there were pestilential vapours and poisonous snakes and herbs.' Secondly, the capital of the Chinese Empire then and, indeed, till the time of the Mongols was at Chan An in the north-west, which was more easily accessible by the north-eastern route. The eastern route took the traders to Szechuan, an important trading area but far away from the political and cultural centre of the empire. The intervening territory was mostly occupied by uncivilized tribes. In consequence, the Central Asian route soon over-shadowed the routes through the north-east.

The route across Tibet developed at a later period and was not important from a commercial point of view.

The last important route to China was by sea. The maritime routes to the Pacific Ocean were known to the coastal peoples of India from the earliest periods of history. As during the 1st century of the Christian era we have allusions in Chinese records to the existence of Hinduized kingdom in what is now known as Indo-China, where the Chinese had also penetrated, the two civilizations may be said to have confronted each other there at least from that time. There was a continuous intercourse between the ports of India and these Hinduized states and also directly between the Indian ports and south China, and Ptolemy, though vague about China, mentions Kattigara as the great port of south China.

There were thus three main lines of communication– across Central Asia by many different routes, via Bamiyan and Bactriana; via Kashgar across the Tarim Valley; and via Kashmir, Gilgit and Yasin across the Pamirs. These routes became important after the 2nd century BC, and till the middle of the 9th century AD, when Islam interposed an effective barrier, they continued to be the most important highways of communication. The earliest route via Assam and Burma never fell into actual disuse, though it lost much of its importance for India as a whole after the growth of traffic across Central Asia. The sea communications grew continuously in importance, especially for South India and, till the blockade of the Chinese coast by the Portuguese, were of the highest importance to Sino-Indian relations. In South Indian literature of the 13th and 14th centuries, junks and sampans are frequently mentioned. From Quilon on the west coast, ships sailed regularly to the ports of south China and it is in one of these that Archbishop Montecorvino travelled to the Far Fast. The last visit of Cheng Ho's armada to the ports of South India was in I424.

When did India first come into contact with its great neighbour? Earlier European scholars had popularized the view that the first contact could not have been before the establishment of the Ch'in dynasty by Shih Huang Ti or the first emperor in 221 BC. They based their argument mainly on the fact that 'Cheena,' by which name the country is known in Indian literature, came probably from Ch'in, representing the new imperial dynasty. But this argument has little value because the word Sinim for China appears in the Old Testament in passages which are considerably older. Also, scholars have pointed out that the word for lion, which was current long before the Ch'in dynasty, was derived from the Sanskrit word *simha*. There is also the tradition, which we have no reason to disbelieve, that the missionaries of Asoka penetrated to the Chinese capital. Though, therefore, no specific date can be given for the discovery of China by India, it would, I think, be correct to say that India was is contact with the south-western regions of China from the earliest period of history but that after the establishment of the Ch'in Empire and the unification of the country the intercourse became much closer; and further, that when in the territories between the north-west of China and the Gandhara region the Kushans built up a great state which was followed by a number of Indianized kingdoms in that area, the relations developed on a regular basis with fruitful results for over a thousand years.

It is only with the introduction of Buddism that we get firm chronological data. The official date for the introduction of Buddhism into China is the year 2 BC. But even before this, the religion of Sakyamuni had penetrated into the Middle Kingdom. Ch'in Shih Huang Ti, the first emperor, is said to have imprisoned an itinerant Buddhist preacher a little more than two hundred years before this date. In the 2nd century BC, the conquering general of the Han Emperor Wu, Ho Puching is said to have taken away some golden statues of the Buddha from the northern tribes when he attacked them. Another tradition recorded in Chinese books is that the religion was unsuccessfully preached in 6 BC. There is no doubt that by the 1st century of the Christian era small Buddhist communities were in existence in the capital itself.

Here, again, it may be recalled that it was not only through one route that Buddhism reached China. It is recorded that one of the Chinese princes who was exiled to the southern provinces received his ordination from a Buddhist community in Kwantung. Dr. Hu Shih, the eminent Chinese scholar, mentioned in a conversation with me that his researches had convinced him that the earlier contacts of Buddhism with China were through the southern route. Later, no doubt, with the more extensive relations established through the Indo-Buddhist kingdoms of Central Asia, the southern influence seems to have become less important. But that it did not at any time cease to act is proved by the existence in Szechuan of Sanskrit inscriptions and the continuing influence of Tantric worship in south-western China.

In the early centuries of the Christian era, Chinese trade with India seems to have assumed considerable proportions. Kalidasa speaks of towns decorated with Chinese silk and the allusion to silk is so common that a very large volume of trade must have developed in that commodity alone.

Because of the sea route, the trade with South India developed separately. Also, unlike the position in north India, intermittent diplomatic relations were also established between the South Indian courts and the Chinese Empire. According to Paul Pelliot, there is evidence in Chinese literature of such intercourse as early as the 2nd century BC. A Chinese writer, Pan Kou, who lived at the end of the 1st century, mentions that in the time of the Han emperor the Chola kings sent embassies to China. The route given by him as well as the name of the state indicates that the kingdom mentioned by him is Kanchi. It is also stated that Wang Ming, the so-called socialist ruler (1st century AD), sent costly presents to the King of Kanchi. Pan Kou says that, from the kingdom of Houang-tch (Kanchi), 'going by boat for about eight months we reach Pi-tsong [an island on the west coast of the Malay Peninsula]'. Travelling again by sea for about two months we get to the frontier of Sianglin in Je-nam [Upper Annam].' Pan Kou also mentions that the exports from South India were 'shining pearls, rare gems and strange products' which the Chinese received in exchange for silk and gold. Pan Kou makes it clear that these journeys were on non-Chinese (Indian) ships.

Just as the Hinduized kingdoms of Khotan and Kuchi were the areas where China and India met and exchanged their cultures in the Central Asian region, it was the Hinduized kingdoms of Funan, Champa, Kamboja and Sri Vijaya that constituted the areas of cultural interpenetration in the Far East. Fortunately, we have more detailed knowledge of these kingdoms than we possess of the states of Central Asia. Mainly owing to the fact that they were not subjected to a violent break with their past through Islamic conquest and conversion, the Indian tradition, Hindu and Buddhist, is a living one in Champa (modern Siam) and Kamboja, while even in Malaya, Sumatra and Java its influence remains clearly marked, in spite of being overlaid with Islam.

There is some reason to believe that the first Indian settlement in the area of Indo-China was established before the beginning of the Christian era. In any case, by the 1st century AD there were to be found in the valley of the Mekong and along the coast of Indo-China a number of Indian principalities. The establishment of the kingdom of Funan in Annam is associated with a Brahmim of the Kaundinya gotra and this event is generally placed in the 1st century AD. The kingdom of Kamboja (Cambodia), also Hindu in religion, using Sanskrit as its official language, was in close diplomatic communication with the court of China from at least the 3rd century AD. The people of Kamboja were mainly emigrants from India who seemed to have reached there by a land route, from Takola mart in Malaya. This route has recently been excavated by Quaritch Wales, whose volume, *The Way to Ankor*, brings together the evidence to establish that there was a continuous connection between the mainland of India and the states of Funan, Champa and Kamboja, which lasted till at least the 15th century.

Apart from the states in the valleys of the Menang and the Mekong where a great Indian civilization flourished for over 1500 years, the Empire of Sri Vijaya striding the straits of Malacca was also a major factor in the maintenance of Sino-Indian relationships. We need not concern ourselves with the question which has agitated historians as to whether the Sri Vijaya capital was at Palembang in Sumatra or at some spot on the Peninsula. Wherever the capital was situated, the territories of Sri Vijaya included both the Malay Peninsula and Sumatra and, in the days of its glory, also a major portion of Java. For over seven hundred years this state, orthodox in its Indian tradition, controlled communications between the Indian Ocean and the Pacific and was the intermediary in the cultural and commercial traffic between India and China. Its relations with India were of the most intimate kind. We know for example that the Sri Vijaya kings endowed institutions in Nalanda and had monasteries erected at their expense in Negapatam. Sanskrit was the official language of the country and most of the old epigraphic records of this kingdom are in that language. The Sailendra monarchs of Sri Vijaya enjoyed great prestige in India and their envoys frequently visited Indian courts.

Also, from the point of view of culture, Sri Vijaya was a genuine projection of India. I-tsing, the famous Chinese pilgrim whose account of his travels, edited by the Japanese scholar Takakusu, constitutes an invaluable mine of information, stayed in Sri Vijaya at different times, the first time for six months during his outward journey, a second time for four years (AD 684-688) on his way back. He was so impressed with the facilities available for study in Sri Vijaya that he returned there, after a short stay in China, for further studies. According to him, the scholars in Sri Vijaya 'investigate and study all subjects just as in India [Madhya Desa]. The rules and ceremonies are not at all different. If a Chinese priest wants to go to the West [India] in order to hear and read [study] he had better stay here and practise the proper rules and then proceed.'

With China also the relations of Sri Vijaya were very close. There were regular sailings from the Sri Vijayan ports to south China. Diplomatic relations were also not uncommon.

Thus, with the vast intervening area between south China and the Bay of Bengal studded with Indianized kingdoms, the trade relations between the two great countries developed normally and without serious interruption. Dr. Caldwell notices in the second half of the last century that many places in south India were 'covered with broken tiles and remnants of Chinese pottery. Hoards of Chinese coins have been discovered in many places in the Tamil country.' Ma Twan Lin, a Chinese historian, speaks of the flourishing trade that esisted between south India and China in the 6th century AD. The exports from India were coral, conches, pearls and ivory. In 1942, coins belonging to the Tang period were discovered in the Tanjore District. In the period of the great Cholas (8th–12th centuries) the relations with China were even more intimate. Embassies were not unusual and one Chinese emperor, hard pressed at the time be the combined forces of the Arabs and the Tibetans, even seems to have sought an alliance with the Chola king. A Chinese Commissioner of Foreign Trade, Chau Ju Kua, compiled a work known as *Chu-fau Chi* in 1225. He describes the different states of India without ever having visited the country, showing the extent of knowledge prevalent in commercial circles in China at the time. Speaking of Kerala, for example, Chau Ju Kua says that its perals, cotton cloth, etc., are taken to a port on the Perak Coast in the Sri Vijaya country where the traders exchanged them for Ho-chi silk, porcelain ware, camphor, etc. Speaking of Quilon, then a great entrepot for trade with China, he says that every year ships come from Sri Vijaya to this port.

We have also evidence of diplomatic relations of South Indian states with China. Allusion has already been made to Pan Kou's statement about the early Cholas. Chavannes, the distinguished French Sinologist, has collected from a Chinese encyclopaedia of the 11th century the references to such embassies in ancient times. The first important embassy mentioned by name is from a western-Indian king by the name of Siladitya whose ambassadors reached the Chinese courth in AD 962. The Pallava emperor, Narasimha Varman Raja Simha, exchanged ambassadors with the Chinese court in AD 720 and seems to have been sounded by the Chinese monarch about the possibility of an alliance. With the Cholas also, the same relations were maintained.

With the fall of the Sri Vijaya Empire in the 14th century and the occupation of the river mouths and ports of Malaya by Muslim navigators, the direct relations between peninsular India and China came practically to an end. A further spurt in China-India trade relations along this route developed under the Ming dynasty, when in I405 Cheng Ho for the first time led a fleet into the Indian Ocean. Successive expeditions followed, the last one being in I430. So, for as long a period as 25 years great Chinese junks were a familiar sight in Indian ports. There are some stray allusions to junks and sampans in the Malayalam poetry of the period.

Cheng Ho's expeditions were organized on an immense scale. His expedition into the Indian Ocean consisted of 62 vessels, each vessel being 440 feet by 180. No less than 37,000 soldiers were carried by this armada. One extremely important result of this formidable enterprise was that the islands of Indonesia and the States of Malaya accepted Chinese suzerainty. So far as India itself was concerned, we have ample descriptions from two men who accompanied these expeditions, Fei Shin and Ma Huan, of the coastal states of India and of the commodities available there for trade.

With the arrival of the Portuguese, the sea route was practically closed to Indian, Arab and Chinese vessels. For the next four centuries, however, India's connection with China did not absolutely cease. But the intermediaries were the Europeans. It is only in the early 19th century that Indian merchants again appear in the Chinese ports, but this time under the protection of the British flag. The great Parsi houses of Bombay, especially the Camas, participated in the Chinese trade and small Indian trading communities came to be established at Canton, Shanghai and Tientsin and other treaty ports. But they were merely subsidiary to British trade and could not be said to have materially contributed to the relations between China and India.

II

Between the 5th and the 10th centuries, for a period over five hundred years, when the land routes were open and the great Hinduized kingdoms of Central Asia were flourishing, the exchange between India and China in the cultural field assumed extraordinary proportions. Large numbers of Chinese visited India regularly as pilgrims, students, etc. Some of them were men of great distinction and their travels in India are well known. In fact, every schoolboy in India knows the names of Fa Hien, Yuan Chuan and I-tsing. But India does not know anything of the great number of very distinguished Indian scholars who spent their lives in China, translating Indian books, teaching in monasteries and generally propagating Indian thought. It is with them that I propose to deal here.

The earliest Indian scholar to reach China of whom we have a record is Kashyapa Matanga who was in China in AD 65. The story of his coming to China is as follows: Emperor Ming of the Eastern Han had a vision of a golden man flying into his palace and his courtiers interpreted the dream as indicating the Buddha. The emperor, anxious to know more about the Buddha and his teachings, sent an embassy to India to bring him the scriptures of Buddhism and some priests of that religion. The embassy returned, bringing with them Kashyapa Mahatma and Dharma Ratna. Maspero has collected no less than thirteen accounts of this legend and according to Pelliot this is not exhaustive. Whatever the truth of the story, there is no doubt that Kashaypa Matanga and Dharma Ratna reached Loyang in

AD 65. Both the monks came from central India. The main work of Kashyapa Matanga is a treatise entitled the 'Sutra of Forty-two Sections'. There are four other works attributed to him but they have been lost.

It is interesting to note that 'The Sutra of Forty-two Sections' is not a translation. The time for the translation of the great classics had not yet come. What Matanga and his collaborator did was to compose an original work on the essentials of Buddhism in order to enable the Chinese to familiarize themselves with its main doctrines.

The next figure, one of the best remembered and the most notable Indian scholars of the day, was Kumarajiva (end of the 4th century). Between the time of Kashyapa Matanga and Kumarajiva, Indian culture had penetrated into China both from the north and from the south. The southern tradition was represented by a remarkable Chinese monk, Meu Tsan, who, in the middle of the 2nd century AD, became a Buddhist during his stay in Tonkin and returned to his country to preach the religion. A southern school deriving its inspiration from the Hinduized kingdoms of Indonesia, Funan, Champa, etc., had established itself firmly in Nanking. A great deal of literature was translated by this school, the most important of which is the translation of the *Avadana Satak*a by Chi Chien. From the northern side scholars both from India and from Khotan and Kuchi were equally busy in translating texts. One of these, a Yue-Chi named Dharma Raksha who had travelled widely in India and learned Sanskrit, translated no less than 211 works into Chinese in the period between AD 284-313. Among his works may be mentioned a translation of the *Lahita Vistara*. It is thus when the taste for Indian literature had already spread a great deal that Kumarajiva made his entry on the Chinese stage.

Kumarajiva was the son of an Indian scholar from Kashmir by a Kuchean princess. Kumarayana, his father, had established himself in Kuchi as a great scholar and there he had married Jiva, the sister of the reigning king. The date of his birth is placed around AD 343. His mother, formerly a nun, started him in his career as a Buddhist priest at the age of·7. At the age of 9 she took him to Kashmir and entrusted his schooling to Bandhu Datta. Bandhu Datta was a celebrated *sarvastivadin* and from him Kumarajiva had his first training in Buddhist doctrines. Three years later, when he was only 12, he met Buddha Yasas at Kashgar and was converted to the Mahayana doctrine. Kumarajiva was a student of the *Vedas* also (W. Liebenthal, *The Book of Chao*, p. 67). Thus he had as a young man mastered both Hindu and Buddhist learning.

After completing his studies, Kumarajiva returned to Kuchi. There he achieved an international reputation as a scholar, teacher and expounder of Buddhist doctrines. The Tsin Emperor, Fu Kien, was so impressed by the fame of umarajiva that he sent an envoy, Po Chuen, to ask the Kuchi king to send Kumarajiva to the Imperial Court. The natural reluctance of the ruler of Kuchi was resented by the Chinese envoy who declared war on the king and, after defeating him, forcibly carried away the monk of China. In 385, Kumarajiva, then over 45, reached China. But it was not all smooth sailing. The Emperor Fu Kien had been murdered and in the interregnum that followed the general who had captured Kumarajiva kept the monk with himself. It was only in 401, when he was nearly 80, that Kumarajiva reached Chang An, the imperial capital.

The Book of Chao, one of the most notable classics of Chinese Buddhism, gives the following description of Kumarajiva's arrival in China:

> The Indian Sramana Kumarajiva, as a small boy, ventured into the vast field of Mahayana, desiring to get to the root of things. He alone rose above the surface of words and symbols; in a mysterious way he entered "the plain region beyond the senses". He quietened the divergent schools ... he fanned the

> pure breeze [of the law] towards the East. Willing to carry his candle further he [was forced to] hide his light in the country of Liang. *Tao* does not work without design; when it works there is purpose. (*The Book of Chao*, p. 68.)

The period of his enforced stay with the general must have been of some value to Kumarajiva in perfecting his knowledge of Chinese. Son of a great Hindu scholar, he was from childhood at home in Sanskrit. Further, he had spent many years in Kashmir, his father's homeland, studying under great masters. Finally, under Buddha Yasas he had achieved a mastery of the classics. In Kuchi, where he was born, he had already become familiar with Chinese and he had now an opportunity of correcting the imperfections of the provincial dialect during his sixteen years stay in Kansu as the guest of the general. Therefore, when he arrived at the Imperial Court he was equally at home in classical Sanskrit and in Chinese, and therefore an ideal interpreter of Indian culture to China.

Emperor Yo Chang accorded him unusual honours. He was made the Raj Guru or Kuo Shih. He preached often before the emperor and enjoyed immense prestige. For the next twelve years, till his death in 413, Kumarajiva was engaged in translating Buddhist texts and correcting earlier translations. During the three centuries before this period an immense literature on Buddhism had developed in China, but the translations were either by Khotanese or Kuchean scholars who knew Sanskrit imperfectly, or by Indian scholars whose knowledge of Chinese was not of a high standard. The local Buddhist converts who had helped the Indian and Kuchean scholars in the work of translation were naturally unfamiliar with Indian ways of thought and, as a result of all these factors, generally speaking the translations were unintelligible to Chinese readers. This is what Kumarajiva set out to remedy. An immense bureau of translators was established under Kumarajiva's supervision with over eight hundred scholars on the staff. In this way over 106 words, including most of the Mahayana texts, were translated. Of these, fifty-six are now available.

Though Kumarajiva had begun as a follower of Hinayana he had, in the course of his stay in Kashmir, become a staunch Mahayanist under the influence of a remarkable guru, Surya Sena, who was then propagating Nagarjuna's teachings in the Kashmir Valley. Till Kumarajiva's time, Chinese Buddhism seems to have been mainly of the Hinayana school. It is Kumarajiva's apostolate in China that established Mahayana as the dominant school of Chinese Buddhism and, consequently, that was responsible for the spread of that school in the Far East. From that point of view alone, Kumarajiva's ministry may well be said to be an event of the highest historical significance.

It is the *prajna* literature, associated with Subhuti, a direct disciple of the Buddha, that forms the basis of Mahayana. Kumarajiva translated five *prajna* works into Chinese and laid the foundation of Mahayana thought. The *Prajna Paramita Hridaya* especially, a short text which most scholars even today know by heart, made the doctrine popular. He followed this up with the translation of the works of Nagarjuna, the great exponent of the Madhyamika school of philosophy and one of the greatest names in Mahayana literature. Nagarjuna and his disciple, Arya Deva, may be considered the Restorers of Mahayana. The *Madhyamika Karika* of Nagajuna with Arya Deva's commentary constitutes the basis of the school. These Kumarajiva and his disciples translated into Chinese. Another translation of Kumarajiva, that of the *Saddharma Pundarika*—'The Lotus of the Good Law' —deserves special mention. No book is so popular with Chinese Buddhists today as the *Saddharma Pundarika*.

Kumarajiva was fortunate in his disciples, especially in Seng Chao who was counted as one of his chief disciples even at the early age of 19 and 'held the brush for him', that is took down his dictation. *The Book of Chao*, one of the more important independent works of Chinese Buddhism, referred to earlier, embodies his teachings.

The greatness of the work of Kumarajiva consists first in his having established a Buddhist literary tradition in China which made the translations easily intelligible to all readers, and thereby more or less naturalized it in China; secondly in his having established a school of translators well-versed in Sanskrit idiom; and thirdly in his having given to Buddhism in China a philosophic basis which has endured in spite of many changes.

Kumarajiva was not merely a translator; he was an original thinker of great genius. He is quoted by one of his disciples as saying: 'If I should write an *abhidharma* of Mahayana it would be better that of Katyayaniputra. Now in the country of Chin where the well-learned men are scare, I am a bird with clipped wings, for scholarly works are of no use here.' What was required in China was not a new treatise, however excellent, but translations of classics in an understandable literary style. It is to this useful but not very original work that he resigned himself. His only original work is a small treatise on *Tatwa* in two chapters. There is also a commentary on the *Vimalakirti Sutra,* which was taken down from his discourses. Kumarajiva may thus be considered to be one of the greatest Indians of all time, one who has left his mark on the history of the Far East. His is a name that everyone in India should cherish.

Another outstanding Indian personality who worked and lived in China at this time was Dharma Kshema who hailed from central India. Originally brought up in the Hinayana doctrine, he, like Kumarajiva, became a Mahayana doctrine, he, like Kumarajiva, became a Mahayanist. His fame as a teacher spread so fast that a Hun monarch in the northern region of China invited him to his court. The king accepted Buddhism and requested Kshema to translate the books which he considered canonical. After a prolonged study of Chinese he undertook the translation of the *Mahaparinirvana Sutra* and many other important works. A rivalry between the Hun king and the Chinese king of Wei for the possession of the learned monk led, it is sorry to relate, to his assassination in 434 by his old patron.

Dharma Kshema is said to have translated altogether twenty-five works, though only twelve of them are now available. Of these, the collection known as the *Maha Sannipata,* a canonical text of great importance to Mahayana Buddhism, translated in full by him, is of the greatest value. Another work of special interest to us which Kshema translated was Aswa Ghosha's famous *kavya, Buddha Charita.* It is interesting to note that while the Sanskrit text of Ashwa Ghosha's *kavya* has only seventeen cantos, the Chinese version has twenty-eight. Also, while the Sanskrit version ends with the Buddha's ministry in Banaras, the Chinese version takes the story up to the *parinirvana* of the Buddha and the distribution of the sacred relics. Kshema's translation could only have been based on a Sanskrit original; but presumably the second portion of the *Maha Kavya* has been lost.

The next personage we shall notice here is Paramartha, a monk born of a Brahmin family of Ujjain, whose work in China rivals that of Kumarajiva. Paramartha had left his home-town and established himself at Pataliputa, where he achieved great fame as an expounder of the *Dharma.* At this time, Emperor Wu Ti had sent a mission to the Magadha king requesting him to send a learned scholar from India to propagate the religion. Paramartha was the person selected. He travelled by sea and reached Nanking in 546. There he was accommodated in the imperial palace and treated with the highest respect. But at that time the Empire was going through a period of political unrest and Paramartha had to leave the royal palace and seek shelter with a local official in the south. He worked in China in different monasteries till 569, that is for a period of twenty-three years and translated over 70 works, of which more than thirty-two are extant. Takakusu, the great Japanese scholar, says of him:

> His teaching embodied a variety of subjects, but throughout, as a Mahayanist, he laid earnest and persistent emphasis on the Buddhistic idealism (*Vijnanvada*) of Vasu Bandhu and Asanga. He seems to have been successful in popularizing the doctrine, for at one time the court is said to have considered the propagation of his idealism as dangerous to the nation. He himself was not satisfied with his work as a preacher of peace. He once said to one of his pupils: "My original plan for which I came here will never be realized. We can entertain at present no hope of seeing the prosperity of the *Dharma.*" But his work as a translator was simply brilliant and in every way satisfactory. We have to thank him for the preservation of several important texts, such as the fundamental works of the Vijnana Vadins, Vasu Bandhu and Asanga, the *Sankhya Karika* of Isvara Krishna with its commentary, besides some works of Nagarjuna, Aswa Ghosha, Vasu Mitra and Guna Mati. What we value most is his biography of Vasu Bandhu, which furnishes us with several otherwise unknown data and sheds an unexpected light on a dark period in the history of Buddhism of the *Sankhya* school and of Indian literature in general.*

One achievement of Paramartha which deserves special notice is his translation of the *Sankhya Karika* into Chinese, together with a comprehensive commentary. In his Introduction Paramartha acknowledges that it is the work of the heretical *rishi* Kapila and not a Buddhist text. Isvara Krishna, a Brahmin, summarized the teachings of Kapila in seventy-two *karikas*. It is this specifically Hindu work, not in any way associated with Buddhism, that Paramartha, who before his conversion was a Brahmin scholar of repute, translated into Chinese. Takakasu holds the view, and has

---

* *Journal of the Royal Asiatic Society*, 1905, p. 33. Article on Paramartha's Life of Vasu Bandhu.

tried to establish by a detailed study, that the *Bhushya* of Gaudapada, the teacher of Sankara, was borrowed wholesale from a *vrithi* of the *Karika* which Paramartha translated into Chinese.

A revolutionary teacher who is still greatly honoured in China and is the subject of many legends is Bodhi Dharma, who belonged to a royal family of Kanchipuram in South India. Bodhi Dharma was not interested in dogmatics or in sacred texts and preached boldly the doctrine that the only reality is the Buddha-nature in the heart of man, and the realization of that Buddha-nature can only come direct experience and not by learning or asceticism. This was the first introduction of Hindu mysticism in a Buddhist garb into China. When Bodhi Dharma was presented at court, he told the emperor that temples and books were of no great value and that inner realization alone could ensure happiness. This was the perennial philosophy which had been preached from the time of the Vedic *rishis*. The emperor asked Bodhi Dharma to explain the holy doctrines. He replied that where all is emptiness, nothing can be holy. The emperor was displeased but the self-realized teacher was not intimidated. Many miraculous acts were attributed to him, such as the crossing of the Yangtse river on a leaf, a popular theme in Chinese painting.

The doctrine of direct inner experience through contemplation found many votaries among the Chinese and the Dhyana school known in Chinese as Chan was the outcome. This is the only live school outside tantricism which has adherents in China. As Zen it spread to Japan where it still holds sway. Eliot, the historian of Hinduism and Buddhism, thus describes the work of Bodhi Dharma:

> The arrival of Bodhi Dharma in Canton in 520 was a great event for the history of Buddhist dogma, although his special doctrines did not become popular until much later. He introduced the Dhyana school and also the institution of the Patriarchate which for a time had some importance. He wrote

> no books himself, but taught that true knowledge is gained in meditation, by intuition, and communicated by transference of thought.... All that a man needs is to turn his gaze inward and see the Buddha in his own heart. This vision which gives light and deliverance comes in a moment. It is a simple, natural act, like swallowing or dreaming, which can not be taught or learnt, but an experience of the soul, and teaching can only prepare the way for it. Some are impeded by their *karma* and are physically incapable of the vision whatever their merits or piety may be, but for those to whom it comes, it is inevitable and convincing.

The Dhyana school which he founded, known as Chan and Zen, is something beyond the intellect. As Aldous Huxley says in *The Perennial Philosophy:*

> In the last analysis, the use and purpose of reason is to create the internal and external conditions favourable to its own transfiguration by and into spirit. It is the lamp by which it finds the way to go beyond itself.

Dr. Coomaraswamy describes Zen Buddhism as 'being little determined by special forms and can scarcely be said to have any other creed than that the Kingdom of Heaven is in the heart of man.' This school of thought, he adds, most fully represents Mahayana as a world religion.

Most of what we know of Bodhi Dharma is derived from two books, the first, *Biographies of High Priests* by Tao-hsuan, compiled in 645, and *The Records of the Transmission of the Lamp*, written in 1004, but based on contemporary records. According to these records, Bodhi Dharma lived in the Shao Lin Monastery and meditated in silence for nine years. There a distinguished Chinese scholar, Shen Kuang by name, came to him and was, after trial, received by him as a disciple. To him, Bodhi Dharma handed the *Lankavatara Sutra* as containing the essence of his message. Shen Kuang who was the second patriarch under the name Hri Ka established the Chan sect on a firm basis. To those who are interested in a modern exposition of this great and influential sect I would strongly recommend Christmas Humphreys' book, *Zen Buddhism.*

Though there were numerous other Indian thinkers and scholars of great note whose biographies are recorded by the Chinese, I shall deal only with one other personage, as representing a separate school. This is Vajrabodhi who introduced the *Mantra Sastra* into China. Vajrabodhi was a Brahmin from Kerala who had attained sufficient eminence in Hindu sciences to become the *guru* of the King of Kanchi. He seems late in life to have been converted to Tantric Buddhism and went to Nalanda at the end of the 7th century for further studies in that university. After some years there he, with his chief disciple, Amogha Vajra, left for China by sea, reaching there in 719, in his 58th year.

The Mantra sect which Vajrabodhi established was tantric esoterism, based on *mula mantras,* and on worship of Devi through *Yantras* or diagrams as practised among the Saktas in India. Its Buddhist counterpart is generally in the Vajra Yana form. Its doctrines and practices and those of other mantra cults are secret, and during Vajrabodhi's eighteen years in China he initiated only two monks into the mysteries of the tantric rituals. But his principal disciple, Amogha Vajra, gave initiation more freely with the result that the demand for tantric texts became widespread and Amogha Vajra was sent on a special mission to collect as many tantric works as possible. As he himself says:

> From my boyhood I revered my late teacher [Vajrabodhi] for ten years and received his instruction in Yoga. Then I went to five parts of India and collected several sutras and sastras, more than five hundred different texts which had not been previously brought to China. In AD 746 I came back to the capital. From that year to the present time I have translated seventy-seven works.

It will be seen from the above short account that it was not only Buddhism that penetrated into China. Sankhya, tantra sastra and other Hindu beliefs were also introduced into the thought of that country. How much of Hinduism was included in this vast export of ideas may be seen from the fact that in the vast collection which Dr. Raghuvira recently brought back from China there is a 3rd century summary of the Ramayana story. Most of the Mahayana scholars seem to have been from among the Hindu *literati,* often Brahmins, and they introduced in their teachings, perhaps unconsciously, many Hindu conceptions. In fact, in the great revival of Buddhist thought in India, beginning with Nagarjuna and Asanga, the distinction between Hindu and Buddhist thought seems gradually to have become blurred.

Another source of Hinduization was through Tibet. In the middle of the 6th century, Srong Tsang unified the clans of Tibet and made it a powerful state. It is he who started Tibet on a career of expansion. His son, Srong Tsang Gampo, annexed Ko Konor and parts of Assam. Though a great conqueror, he was also a great reformer. He introduced into Tibet a modified Indian alphabet based on Nagari. His Nepalese wife is said to have introduced the cult of Tara into Tibet. Many Sanskrit books were translated into Tibetan in his time. But it was in the reign of Srong Be Tsan (740-786) that Indian cultural dominance became well established. He invited numerous Indian scholars to Tibet, notably Santa Rakshita (747), who became his *guru.* It was at his suggestion that the great Padma Sambhava, known as Guru Rimpoche, the precious teacher, was invited to Tibet.

Another stream of Hinduization has recently been brought to light by the explorations of Guiseppe Tucci.* It would appear that at the end of the 12th century some Hindu tribes moved into Western Tibet and established there a kingdom with Senija or Sija as its capital. The dynasty which

---

* G. Tucci, 'Preliminary Report of Two Scientific Expeditions to Nepal', Rome, ISMEO, 1956.

established this kingdom is known as the Mallas, to be differentiated from the later family of Mallas who ruled over Nepal. The first king of this dynasty was Nagaraja who is alluded to in the Tibetan chronicles as Nagadeva. This kingdom seems to have prospered for about three hundred years, attaining a degree of imperial power under Prithivi Malla whose sway seems to have extended not only to Western Tibet and portions of Nepal, but also to some areas on the side of India proper. Though the descendants of Nagadeva originally adopted Buddhism, by about the middle of the 18th century a process of Hinduization seems to have set in. Ripu Malla, one of Prithivi Malla's ancestors, according to Tibetan sources conquered some of the sub-Himalayan valleys on the Indian side and thereby established direct trade and cultural contacts with Hindustan. In any case from his time there was, according to Tucci, 'slow but constant penetration of Hinduism, the Hinduization of the Court and consquently of the upper classes.' From one of the records of Pratapa Malla (written in AD 1376), Brahma, Vishnu and Maheswara are invoked along with the Buddha, Dharma and Sangha. The beginning and end of this record is in Sanskrit, written in the ornate style of the Champu Kavya. The name of the composer of the record in given as Sivadeva.

The existence for over a period of three hundred years of a powerful kingdom on the northern side of the Himalayas as an outpost of Hindu culture must have inevitably led to the spread of Hindu influence in Tibet. When the Malla empire disappeared, this Hindu influence did not cease altogether. With the breakdown of Rajput power in Rajasthan, some of the chiefs seem to have penetrated into this region. According to Tucci,

> The records mention that the new chieftains came from Rajasthan, a few courageous leaders with a few followers who conquered new possessions for them in sub-Himalayan countries. The name of Chitor recurs very often in these

> documents: that these chiefs claimed such a descent is known also to the Tibetans and a mention of this claim is contained in Tibetan records.*

Padma Sambhava was the founder of the Tantric sect of Buddhism in Tibet. Tibet became the land of great monasteries under his inspiration. As at this period Tibet's political authority extended to parts of western China and Mongolia, Tibetan tantricism obtained a great hold on the border nationalities of China. In the Yuan or Mongolian period, Lamaism became a fashion as the emperor himself accepted the creed. The Tibetan monk, Phago-pa, was invited to the Mongol court in 1256, by Kubilai Khan. Kubilai made him Raj Guru and recognized him as the head of the Buddhist Church. It is he who invented the alphabetic system for the Mongol language. This position of influence continued even under the Manchus. Thus it can be said that the mission of the great intermediate states of Khotan, Kuchi, etc. which had vanished was in a measure taken up by Tibet (see Appendix I). But there was a basic differences. The Buddhism that reached China, Mongolia and other countries through Tibet was of the Tantric variety and not the high intellectual creed represented by the philosophies of Asanga, Vasu Bandhu and Aswa Ghosha. Further, it led to a penetration of Hindu, especially Saivite, cults into China, a subject which has so far not been studied at all. In the collection brought back by Dr. Raghuvira there is a banner with the Gayatri mantra written on it in Mongolian characters. Curiously enough, during my stay in Peking some of the houses which the staff of the Embassy occupied were in an area known as Mahakala Miao, the temple of Mahakala. The Saivite element in popular Chinese Buddhism, introduced mainly through the Tantric cults is very noticeable.

---

* Ibid., p. 109.

There is one further point which requires emphasis. It is through the work of these great scholars and the translations they made into Chinese that we know today the names of some of the greatest thinkers and philosophers that India has produced. Nagarjuna, Asanga and Vasu Bandhu are men who are in no way inferior to Sankara and Ramanuja, among the later philosophers, and Iswara Krishna, Gaudapada and others of the earlier period. But even their names would have been forgotten and their views known only by the criticism of their opponents as in the case of Kanada, Charvaka and others if their works had not been translated into Chinese and their biographies preserved in China. Of Nagarjuna, perhaps the greatest of them and the leading philosopher of the Madhyamika school, Dr. Radhakrishnan says:

> We have in Nagarjuna, one of the greatest thinkers of India, a far more vigorous sifting of the contents of experience than we found in either the subjectivist or the realist. He is sustained by an unselfish intellectual enthusiasm and philosophical ardour which aim at thoroughness and completeness for their own sake.... In the true philosophic spirit, Nagarjuna reveals the paradoxes which our everyday consciousness veils by a more or less thoughtless phraseology and indifference to reflection.

This great thinker, who was a South Indian Brahmin by birth and lived probably not later than the 2nd century AD, is known to us mainly by the translations of his works in Chinese and by Kumarajiva's biography, also in Chinese.

About Asanga and Vasu Bandhu also this is equally true. These two great thinkers of the Yogachara school are hardly known to us from any purely Indian sources. It is through the translation of their works into Chinese that they have now been repatriated to India. Another remarkable personage who has been welcomed back in India's pantheon of glory is Aswa Ghosha. Whether the philosopher Aswa Ghosha was the same person as the epic poet who wrote the

Buddha Charita and the *Soundara Nanda* we need not consider here. To me it does not appear that the case for identity has been established. The philosopher would appear to be the more important personality for his *Mahayana Sraddhotpada*, translated by Suzuki as 'The Awakening of the Faith', is a great and germinal work in the Mahayana school. Aswa Ghosha, a Brahmin from eastern India, who lived in the 1st century AD, is said to have been the spiritual preceptor of Kanishka. His philosophical work is now known to us from Chinese texts.

The Indian literature preserved in Chinese is extensive and but for the care with which Indian scholars translated and Chinese scholars preserved this literature, it would have been totally lost to the world.

What I have said above may convey the impression that Indian influence in China was something which had to do essentially with scholars, philosophers and courts. This was far from being the case. The Buddhist religion did not reach China as a system of elaborate metaphysics and spiritual discipline but as

> a form of popular worship and belief gradually taking root among the people, probably the poorest and the most lowly to whom the Buddhist missionaries, traders and travellers had brought the good tidings of mercy and delivery from pain.... The apparently rapid progress made by Buddhism in the Yangtse Valley and on the southern coast towards the end of the 2nd century seems to indicate that it had a long period of slow but steady permeation among the people. By the 3rd century, when the men of letters began to admire and defend it, Buddhism had already become a powerful religion, not because there was governmental patronage of which there was very little, but because of its powerful following among the people.

It was the common man's religion and in continued to be so till our own time.

* * *

So far, we have dealt with some leading Indian thinkers who visited China. The number of Chinese pilgrims and scholars who visited India was of course unusually large. Of these the names of Fa Hien, Yuan Chuan (Hiouen Tsang) and I-tsing are well known and their contributions to Sino-Indian relations need not be discussed here. But there is a general idea that with the downfall of the Tang dynasty and with the interruption of communications through Central Asia, Chinese pilgrims ceased to frequent holy places in India or pursue their studies at Indian centres of learning. That this was not so is amply proved by the Chinese inscriptions discovered at Bodh Gaya. Discussing these inscriptions in the *Revue de l'histoire des Religions* (1896), the famous French scholar Chavannes says:

The Chinese pilgrims who went to India in this period [in the 10th and 11th centuries] were numerous. As early as 964 AD when the Song dynasty had come into power only for five years, 300 monks left for the Holy Land. They travelled for twelve years. One of them named Ki-ye has left a short account of his travels. The year following their departure, the monk Tao-yuan came back from the west after an absence of 18 years. In 966, 156 persons among whom there was one King-k'in responded to an invitation from the Emperor who wanted to send a mission to India. In 978, Ki-ts'ong and his companions came back from India, Kuang-yuan came back in 982, Fa-yu came back in 983 and left again for India just after his return, Ts'e-huan came back between 984 and 987 and Ch'ong-ta who was away from China for ten years returned in 989 (990 ?). Last of all in 1031, Huai-wen, who had gone to India twice, left for India for the third time. He came back in 1039 and it was during this mission that he set up in 1033 an inscription which has been preserved at Bodhgaya.

Besides these men there were certainly others of whom the historians have kept no account. None of the authors of the inscriptions of 1022 is mentioned either in the *Fo-tsu-t'ong-ki* or in the history of the Song dynasty. If they could be forgotten, there is no knowing how many others had shared the same fate. We know besides that there were in 982 a number of Chinese monks at the Imperial Court who knew Sanskrit. It is probable that they had been to India for their studies.

The most important thing is that a good number of these monks did not travel as common men. Some of them had been entrusted by the Emperor with quasi-official missions. The 156 men who left in 966 AD were furnished with letters patent ordering all the kings of Central Asia and Northern India to help them with guides. Similarly Fa-yu who was to follow the route passing by Sumatra about 983 AD had received credentials for the principal kingdoms in that island. On their arrival in India the pilgrims had often to carry out certain religious duties in the name of their Emperor. Kuang-yuan who came back in 982 could prove by a letter from an Indian Prince that he had given on behalf of the Emperor a kasaya to the Buddha at Bodhgaya. Huai-wen was acting directly on behalf of the Emperor Jen-tsong and the Empress in building a stupa at Bodhgaya in 1033 AD. The Indian monk Kio-kie who came to China in 1010 AD was given by the Imperial order a gold embroidered kasaya for presentation at the Vajrasana. Even in the T'ang period, the pilgrims were not entrusted with such missions. The first Song emperors alone used the services of the monks for their personal religious duties.

III

The dominance of Indian thought in China for a period of over six hundred years and the continuance of Buddhism in its naturalized form as one of the principal factors in Chinese life even up to our own time, lead us to the important question of the character and extent of Indian influence. The great Chinese philosopher, a scholar of encyclopaedic knowledge and balanced judgment, Dr. Hu Shih, in a comprehensive article entitled 'The Indianziation of China, A Case Study in Cultural Borrowing', contributed to the Harvard Tercentenary publication has attempted to estimate the different aspects of Indian cultural influence in China. Starting with the statement that 'the long history of Indianization of Chinese institutions, thought, art, and life in general furnishes the most extensive material that can be found for the study of cultural borrowings on the grandest scale', he proceeds to analyse the general nature of cultural borrowings, and comes to the conclusion that, starting with plain borrowing and imitation, the process ends by domestication and appropriation. The stages which mark this process are stated by him to be in the following order:

(1) Mass borrowing
(2) Resistance and persecution
(3) Domestication
(4) Appropriation

Dr. Hu Shih explains these terms as follows:

> By mass borrowing I mean not only the simple process of China's taking from India all those things which were either totally absent or weak in the indigenous civilization but also

> that mass movement of religious enthusiasm which blindly embraced everything that accompanied the new faith. By resistance and persecution I mean to include those periods of history when the invading culture was openly opposed by Chinese thinkers and persecuted by governmental action. By domestication, I mean to include all those tendencies consciously or unconsciously to make the Indian religion, art, thought and institutions take up more and more Chinese colours, in order that the Chinese people may feel more at home in them. By appropriation, I mean the culminating stage of successful borrowing, when the essence, if not the bodily totality of the borrowed culture was unconsciously "appropriated" and recognized by the native population as their own.

Dr. Hu Shih's description of the acceptance of Buddhism by the masses of China in the 4th, 5th and 6th centuries is worth quoting.

> Then there came the great religion of the Buddha together with all the Mahayana trimmings of the pre-Buddhist and non-Buddhist religions of India. Never before had China seen a religion so rich in imagery, so beautiful and captivating in ritualism and so bold in cosmological and metaphysical speculations. Like a poor beggar suddenly halting before a magnificent storehouse of precious stones of dazzling brilliance and splendour, China was overwhelmed, baffled and overjoyed. She begged and borrowed freely from the munificent giver. The first borrowings were chiefly from the religious life of India, in which China's indebtedness to India can never be fully told. India gave China for example not only one paradise but tens of paradises, not only Hell but many hells, each varying in severity and horror from the other. The old simple idea of retribution of good and evil was replaced by the idea of the transmigration of the soul and the iron law of *Karma* which runs through all past, present and future existences. These and thousands of other items of belief and practice have poured from India by land and by sea into China and have been accepted and gradually made into parts of the cultural life of China.

Naturally, with such a people as the Chinese, justly proud of their own long-established civilization, with their distinctive attitude towards life, with their own philosophies, this wholesale acceptance of what was essentially a foreign religion, with its attendant culture, could not proceed for long without strenuous opposition. Such opposition soon developed from the Confucian *literati* who not only defended Confucianism vigorously but counter-attacked Buddhist doctrines, especially the tendency of converts to become monks and to renounce their families and to practise celibacy—both directly opposed to the strong familial tradition of Chinese civilization and its emphasis on both ancestor-worship and on posterity. As a result of this organized counter-attack, Indian influence in China had to face four periods of serious and sustained persecution, in 446, 574, 845 and 955. As Dr. Hu Shih observes, 'it is significant to note that all edicts for the persecution of Buddhism emphasized the fact it was an alien religion and that it was a national disaster and a humiliation for the Celestial Empire to be thus under the influence of aliens.' Han yu (768-824), the intellectual father of the great persecution of 845, coined these concise slogans: 'Restore their people to humanity, burn their books and convert their temples and monasteries to human residences.' These persecutions were on the largest scale imaginable. Thus, speaking of the great persecution of 845, Dr. Hu, after enumerating the temples and monasteries demolished, millions of acres of monastic land confiscated and vast numbers of monks and nuns forced to return to lay life, quotes the Emperor as saying: 'Henceforth all affairs of monks and nuns shall be dealt with by the Bureau of Foreign Affairs', thereby denying them Chinese nationality.

But strange to say such exhibitions of imperial power and nationalist reaction had never more than temporary success. Indian influence had gone too far and had penetrated the masses to such an extent that, whatever the official policy or the orders issued, the movement went on apace.

After the 10th century, however, the religious fervour began to decline. Though Buddhism continued and continues to be a major influence in China, after the 10th century there is a very noticeable weakening of popular enthusiasm. Dr. Hu Shih explains this as being due to the twin process of domestication and assimilation. As an example of domestication he draws our attention to the signification of Indian figures. 'Look at the faces of the deities in a Buddhist temple in China today', he says, 'and trace each to its earliest Indian original and you will realize how this process of domestication has worked. The most striking examples are the various stages of transformation of the god Avalokiteswara, who was long ago unsexed and became the Goddess of Mercy, often represented as a beautiful woman with tiny bound feet. Maitreya has now become the big-bellied, heartily laughing Chinese monk that greets you as you enter any Buddhist monastery in China. Indeed, all faces of the Buddhist deities have been Sinicized through a long but unconscious process of domestication.'

Nowhere can this process be more clearly seen and studied than in the Tunghuan cave paintings, where the art of four centuries can be seen side by side and compared carefully. The first paintings in the caves of the Wei period are distinctly Indian and the figures represent Indian types. Slowly the physiognomy changes till, in the Tang period, the Indian type can only be faintly recognized. In the paintings of the Sung period (12th century), the figures are distinctly Chinese except for the postures, *mudras*, etc.

Dr. Hu Shih shows clearly that this domestication covered every aspect of cultural life, music, painting, architecture, and drama, all of which in due course became Sinicized. Chinese drama, developed from Indian models, later took on an entirely Chinese form.

Indian influence on sculpture and painting is well known and does not require to be restated here. With regard to drama, scholars trace three stages: first when the technique, the story and the characters were borrowed from India. Slowly, while the story and the characters remained Indian, the technique was suitably altered to meet Chinese characters replace the Indian and the story is suitably modified. A new national Chinese drama comes into being in which Indian influences can only be noticed by scholars. So far as music is concerned, the following quotation from a recent issue of *Chinese Literature,* an official publication of the People's Republic, explains the position succintly:

> As early as the Sui dynasty (581-618 AD), Indian music was formally recognized by the Chinese government as one of the chief categories of music. Later, during the Tang dynasty (615-907 AD), the tune of a Brahmin Dance which was introduced into China from the North West became, after a certain amount of modification, the melody of the celebrated Rainbow Garment Dance. This melody was so popular with the Chinese of the Tang dynasty that the famous poet, Pai Chu Yi wrote a poem in praise of it... It is little wonder that when a Chinese audience today hears Indian music they feel that while possessing a piquant Indian flavour it has a remarkable affinity with Chinese music. (4th Issue, 1955, p. 164.)

The influence of Indian astronomy in China was very marked. Gautama Siddha, a Hindu monk, was the guru of I-tsing who was employed by the court in 721 to reform the calendar. Indian books on mathematics were also translated into Chinese and influenced the development of mathematics in China.

The process of assimilation was gradual. In that process China naturally discarded what she could not digest. A process of simplification was necessary, especially in the realm of religion and ideas. This was provided by Bodhi Dharma by his Dhyana school. To quote Dr. Hu Shih again:

> By the 11th century, Zennist Buddhism was more of a philosophy than a religion. But that was what it should be. For was not original Buddhism more a philosophy than a religion? Unconsciously and unwittingly, the Chinese Buddhists, through a long period of a thousand years, had succeeded in shearing Mahayana Buddhism of all its extraneous verbiage and in remaking it into a philosophy and a technique. Unconsciously they had made their Buddhism nearer to primitive Buddhism than any Hinayana or Mahayana sects had ever been. And, incidentally, they had thereby so domesticated Buddhism as to make it easily understood and appreciated by the Chinese intelligentsia.

The final process of assimilation was then the cultural content of Indian influence penetrated Taoism and Confucianism. Its mystical and other-worldly aspects were absorbed in the revived Taoism and Taoist thinking accepted Buddhist categories. The interpretation of Confucianist thought had also a similar and unexpected result. In the 11th century, when the rational philosophy of Neo-Confucianism appeared, the Confucians claimed that it was based on certain neglected aspects of their ancient teachings. However, the historical fact which is now recognized is that this re-inter-pretation was

> the result of one thousand years of Buddhist philosophizing and thinking. Especially, the four hundred years of Zennist Buddhism had given the Chinese philosopher a new set of intellectual habits, a new source of reference material. It was as if the naked eye had been aided by a new eye glass which enabled him to see things which he had been unable to see before. And the eye glass was unfortunately coloured. He now saw things through this eye glass coloured by centuries of Buddhist and Zennist training. He now reinterpreted all he saw in the new light. He was unconsciously appropriating what he had honestly disowned and revolted against.

In fact, the Confucianist revival since the 11th century was essentially an appropriation and assimilation of Indian thought. The conclusions of Dr. Hu Shih are worth quoting:

What had happened during these thousand years to bring about such a tremendous difference in the Chinese outlook on life? Nothing but the gradual deepening and intensifying of the Indianization of Chinese thought, life and institutions. Buddhism was fading away, but its cultural content had been domesticated and appropriated by the secular thinkers and had penetrated into Chinese life and institutions far beyond the confines of the monasteries and nunneries of Buddhism. It is true that, with the dying of religious fanaticism, the perfunctory Buddhist monks no longer burned themselves on altars as sacrifices to Buddha. But China was erecting everywhere stone monuments to encourage young widows never to marry again, and even to encourage young girls to refuse to marry after the death of their fiancés before marriage. And strangely enough, the age of Rational Philosophy coincided with the rapid development and spread of that most inhuman institution of foot-binding which caused untold suffering to the whole of Chinese womanhood for a thousand years—an institution of which the poets sang in enthusiastic praise and against which the philosophers never raised a voice in protest!

> We can only measure the degree of Indianization by comparing this age of moral austerity and self-righteousness with the simple and natural humaneness of pre-Buddhist China. Truly, Indianization had attained its consummation in the hands of the Rational Philosophers, who set out to eradicate the Indian religion by the revival of ancient Chinese thought but unwittingly appropriated the spirit and essence of the very culture they had intended to uproot. In their blind emphasis on the Divine Reason as the opposite of human desire, in their suppression of sex and the simple joys of life, in their righteous indignation against the remarriage of widows, and in their helpless resort to quiet meditation as a moral and intellectual technique—in these and many other aspects these great philosophers of esoteric rationalism were unconsciously acting as the most effective agents for the final Indianization of China.

We have analysed and discussed the thesis of Dr. Hu Shih at some length not only because he is the most eminent thinker of modern China who has devoted a great deal of time and thought to this problem, but also because, in view of his consistent view that Indian influence has been disastrous to the course of China's natural development, he could not be accused of pro-Buddhist views. His main idea that Chinese Buddhism penetrated both the Taoist and Confucian schools and re-incarnated itself in Sinified forms is essentially right and would hardly be questioned. But the explanation of the decay of Buddhism from the 11th century which he provides is only partially true. Other and perhaps more important factors also contributed to the decay of Buddhism. First, the line of communication from India across Central Asia was disrupted in the 8th century and Chinese Buddhism lost its source of inspiration—the large number of scholars and missionaries from India and of the pilgrims from China who returned after prolonged stays in India.

The final disruption of communications between China and India across this great route which provided for an interview exchange for over seven hundred years came in the second half of the 8th century. Islamic expansion from the West began penetrating into Central Asia. At the same time, a formidable military power had arisen in the unaccustomed region of Tibet, a power which was moving into the Tarim Basin. The rise of Tibetan military power at this period is one of the unexplained phenomena of history, but there is no doubt that this small nation was able to wrest large areas from the great Chinese Empire and even occupy the Tunghuan area, where their tantric practices are pictorially represented in many of the later caves. Joining hands with the Arabs from the west, they seem to have been able to push back the Chinese from Central Asia into China proper. The last heroic effort of the Chinese to maintain their position in Central Asia was the campaign of General Kao

Hshien-chih in AD 750. In a brilliantly successful campaign, Kao, with a powerful army, moved across the ice-covered Darkot Pass and occupied Yasin and Gilgit, whose princes were allied to the Tibetans. But a year later his army met with disaster, and with this ended Chinese authority in Central Asia, till its reconquest a thousand years later by Emperor Chan Luen.

This breakdown of Chinese authority in Central Asia was an event of tremendous significance in Sino-Indian relations. Chinese aggression had already destroyed the Indo-Buddhist succession states of the Kushans, Khotan and Kuchi and other kingdoms which had played so notable a part for over six centuries. With the withdrawal of the Chinese, this vital area therefore passed to Islam and an unbridgeable barrier came into existence between India and China in the areas where they had collaborated most fruitfully for so many centuries. That route has remained practically closed ever since.

From the 8th century, the only effective land route between India and China was through Tibet. The period of Tibetan expansion noticed above witnessed the organization of the Himalayan uplands into an ordered state. With the Islamization of Central Asia, this country assumed a special importance in fostering Sino-Indian friendship. The Tibetan kings had themselves become Buddhists and began to welcome Indian scholars and missionaries from Nalanda and Vikramashila. But the route was never paraticularly important and the trade and cultural relations between the two countries languished.

Secondly, by the end of the 10th century, Buddhism had ceased to be a major factor even in North India. The universities of Nalanda and Vikramashila continued to exist, but the great days of Buddhist philosophy were over and were replaced by the growth of a debased form of Tantricism. So the source itself had dried up and the lines of communication had been disrupted even earlier.

Finally, India was herself subjected to violent inroads by Muslims from the north-west. The sea routes had also passed under the control of the Arabs, and the communications of the south with the Far East seem to have been greatly reduced, if not interrupted, at the end of the 10th century. At this time Pallava authority had become unimportant in the south and, in consequence, the contacts with the Buddhist communities of the Far East had languished.

Though the direct propagation of Indian culture through Buddhism and through Buddhist missionaries ceased by the 10th century, it would be a mistake to think that other Indian influences were not reaching China. The intellectual aspects of Buddhism had been assimilated by the *literati* but the masses continued to repeat *sutras* and burn incense before images. Deprived of intellectual leadership, they became a prey to the doctrines of Tantra, while the Tibetan domination of the north-west had introduced in that area and in Mongolia. With the Yuans, themselves originally believers in Shamanism, the Tibetan cults reached the Imperial Court itself. A considerable amount of Saivite and other Hindu influence was absorbed by the common people. Thus a debased Buddhist Hindu thought penetrated across the valley of the Himalayas till quite recent times.

It has been a general complaint of Chinese scholars that Sino-Indian relations during the first millennium of the Christian era was a one-way traffic in which India gave and China received many things, leading so distinguished and objective a scholar as Hu Shih to describe the movement as the Indianization of China. But students of cultural contacts will no doubt recognize that such one-sided influence is never possible. The experience of Asia's contact with Europe, for a much lesser period, provides ample evidence to prove that even the most dominant society cannot fail to be influenced by continuous contact. It is no doubt true that, in the case of China, it is Chinese scholars who studied Indian language, literature and thought, while such Indians as went to China and studied Chinese went there to influence and not to be influenced. And yet the contacts were so vigorous and extended over such a long period that it would be absurd to deny the influence of Chinese civilization on India.

In the economic and material field, it is possible to trace such influence even now. The wide prevalence of silk from very earliest times is attested to by our literature. Fruits of different kinds, especially pears and peaches as noted by Yuan Chuan were introduced from China, as also the lichi which still retains its Chinese name. Professor Bagchi has suggested that vermilion probably came first from China. In the south of India, the technique of the fishing industry in the backwaters seems to have been introduced from Canton. Also, it is well known that a flourishing porcelain industry was introduced into Kerala by the Chinese. In fact, it is known that a small colony of Chinese existed near Quilon for many centuries.

In the field of religion also there has been some influence of Chinese beliefs, especially in areas bordering on China. I have already alluded to Kamakhya worship in Assam. The Chinachara cult, which is recognized as one of the official forms of Tantricism, claims a connection with China. It is difficult to say how far it has been influenced by Taoist mystic discipline but it is obvious from its very name that its origin is Chinese. That at certain periods there was an interest among a section of Indian scholars in Chinese Taoist thought is evidenced by the request of Kumara, King of Kamrup, for a translation of *Tao Ta king.* This request was conveyed to the Chinese envoys who visited his court. The translations were undertaken under the Emperor's orders. Professor Bagchi, our leading authority on these questions, traces some aspects of the *sahajayana* to the influence of these texts. As *sahaja* may be a translation of 'true nature', a doctrine of Taoist philosophy, it may well be that the influence of Taoism was responsible for this development.

But one thing is clear: that the subject of Chinese influences on India has not been studied seriously. It is something which deserves the serious attention of both Indian and Chinese scholars.

Intimate religious, cultural and social relations existed between the two major civilizations of Asia for a period of nearly fifteen hundred years. For nearly a thousand years, from the 1st century BC to the 10th century AD. It was one of the major facts of the world's cultural history. Its importance in shaping the mind of East Asia, including Japan, Korea and Mongolia, is something which cannot be overrated. It created the Asian mind, a community of ideas, beliefs and traditions which even today give to non-Islamic Asia a basic unity, the importance of which is only now being recognized. The contribution of this close association of the Indian and Chinese peoples over so long a period is therefore something which requires continuous and intensive study by us.

After the arrival of the Portuguese, when the sea routes to the countries of Asia were blockaded, this contact, which was fruitful in its results not only for India and China but for the rest of Asia, ceased completely. Now a new period of mutual influence has been born. The lines of communication have been re-formed. India and China confront each other in the modern age ready to learn. This new period will no doubt produce as glorious and enduring civilizations as the previous ones.

Appendixes

Appendix I

Tibet in Sino-Indian Relations

Nepal was always considered an integral part of the wider Hindu life, and though it was able generally to maintain its political independence from the empires of the Gangetic Valley, its cultural unity with India has never been open to question. Equally, from very early times, it has had close relations with Tibet. Till the end of the 6th century AD, the Tibetan uplands had never been united into a single kingdom. At that time a great ruler arose in Tibet in the person of Srong Tsang (died 650) who welded the tribes together into a single state. His son Srong Tsang Gampo, basing his power on the inaccessible heights of Tibet, pressed against both China and Nepal. Both the great Tang emperor and the little Himalayan kingdom followed the same policy in regard to the Tibetan conqueror. The Chinese emperor offered Srong a princess of the imperial house as a consort. The Nepalese monarch gave his own daughter in marriage to him. As Sylvain Levy has put it, 'they [the queens] had each brought away from their country their idols, their rites and their select books.' As both the queens were ardent Buddhists, Tibet was soon converted into a Buddhist country, providing a new though difficult line of communication between India and China.

This route was first opened by a group of pilgrims led by Li i piao. It followed the route which the princess's party had taken in 641, and from Lhasa the party moved down to the Himalayas, crossing the mountain ranges through the Kirong Pass.

The Tibetan state under the successors of Srong Tsang became one of the major powers of Central Asia, annexing portions of Szechuan, the basin of the Kokonor, and pushing its authority into the Tarim Basin and the Tunghuan area. The Tibetan kings seem at this stage to have allied themselves with the growing Muslim power in Central Asia and their combined forces threatened the peace of north-west China.

One of the great achievements of Srong Tsang Gampo was the introduction into Tibet of a modified version of the Indian alphabet. A mission of sixteen scholars under the Minister, Thummi Sambotha, was sent to India to study the system of writing. They evolved a simplified alphabet out of the Devanagri script and introduced it into Tibet in AD 639. Another of his achievements was the composition of a Tibetan grammar based on the principles of Indian grammarians. He also translated the grammar of Panini and Chandra Gomin into Tibetan.

The next great Tibetan king, Kring Sron Ide Btsan (AD 740-786) began the policy of inviting Indian scholars and religious teachers to the kingdom. His own preceptor, Shantarakshita, was a scholar of repute and it was at his suggestion that the king invited the great Padmasambhava and his disciple Vairochana to Tibet.

Padmasambhava is one of the greatest names in Tibetan history. He was a tantric Buddhist and it is mainly through his influence that this form of Buddhism became predominant in Tibet. He founded the Red Hat Sect and built the first large monastery in Tibet, modelled on Odantapuri in Bengal.

From his time the relations between India and Tibet in the field of scholarship and religion were most intimate. Groups of Tibetan scholars were sent to Indian universities, especially to Nalanda, Vikramashila and Odantapuri, and a great movement for the translation of Indian works was set on foot. The movement reached its climax under Dipankar

Srijnana, better known as Atisa, who arrived in Tibet in the year 1042. Atisa did not deny the virtues of Vajrayanism (tantra) but emphasized the doctrines of Asanga and Nagarjuna and based himself on the interpretation of Prajnaparamita texts.

Other Indian sects also reached Tibet at this time, especially a yoga school which, through the practice of Hathayoga and meditation, claimed that man's nature could be perfected and that he could achieve liberation while in this world.

As a result of the political chaos in North India following the invasion of the Gangetic Valley by the Muslims, and especially the break-up of the universities in Bihar, a large number of Indian scholars took refuge in Tibet. It is at this time, when Tibet had thus become a major centre of Indian culture, that political circumstances brought her into the closest contacts with China. In 1206, Genghiz Khan had already demanded and obtained the unconditional surrender of Tibet. In 1239, Goldan, second son of Ogdai, sent a force to Tibet, one result of which was the establishment of the preeminence of the Sa Sakya Abbot in the affairs of the kingdom. The Abbot was able to convert the Mongols to Buddhism, though he was not able to prevent the establishment of their authority.

The Sa Sakya Pandita's letter on his visit to the Mongol Khan's camp is an interesting document, which deserves study:

> Having in mind the Buddha's teaching in general and [the good of] all created beings, and particularly what may be of advantage to the Tibetan-speaking population, I have gone to the Hor. The great patron was much pleased with me, whom he had invited. I had thought that Pagspa who had taken with him his small brother and his retinue would have been enough. But he said to me, "Among my subjects I consider you as the head, the others the feet. You have been called by me, the others

> will come through fear. Do I not know it?"
>
> Before coming here Pagspa and his brother were acquainted with the land of Tibet and even now Pagspa studies the law of Tibet. [He said] I, protecting the world with the law of man, and you, protecting it with the law of man, and you, protecting it with the law of the gods, will the Buddha's teachings spread all over the world as far as the ocean which is the earth's external boundary.
>
> The King is a Bodhisattva who has the greatest faith in the Buddhist teachings generally and in the three great gems in particular. He protects the universe by good laws and particularly he has a great attachment for me far above the others. He said [to me], "Preach religion with a tranquil mind. I will give you what you wish. I know that you do good, heaven knows if I do so also...."

Thus Tibet became a part of the Mongol Empire with the Sa Sakya Pandita as the Mongol agent. He ended his letter by saying:

> I have entered the Mongol confederation with thoughts of love towards others for the advantage of those who speak Tibetan. If you listen to me it will be to your advantage. ... Let the Buddha's teachings be diffused over all the Mongol regions.

Tibet lost its political independence but in the process it gained a spiritual empire.

Under Kublai Khan whose capital was at Peking, the Mongol overlordship was transformed into a Chinese one. The political effects of this transformation need not concern us here; but its spiritual effects were important. In the first place, the entire Mongol area passed under the influence of Tibetan Buddhism. In fact even today, the Mongols, generally speaking, follow the Lamaism of Tibet and are organized under the authority of the great monasteries. Secondly, in the areas of China near Tibet, especially Szechuan and Kokonor, Tibetan tantric Buddhism penetrated, to a great extent displacing the earlier Mahayana forms. When Tibet was again united under the Dalai Lamas this influence became notable, especially under the fifth Dalai who was a great scholar and saint.

From the point of view of Indian cultural contacts, it is important to remember that the Tibetan tantric forms had in many cases become indistinguishable from Hindu tantras. As Professor Tucci says,

> In course of time this tantric literature [in Tibet] developed unrestrictedly, displaying the same luxuriant growth in the Shivaitic and in the Buddhist sects with the natural contaminations and analogies. Both schools interpreted with the same intentions an identical religious enthusiasm, drew their inspiration from the same experiences and gave the same interpretation to the spiritual urge of the masses.... This also explains the inconographic analogy of many of these gods issuing as from an inexhaustible source, out of the exalted imagination of devotees. Buddhism, when it abandons the human form and multiplies the heads and arms of its divinities, copies Hinduism extensively; certain tantric images like Halahalavalokitesvara and Nilakantavalokitesvara clearly are contaminations of Shiva. Brahma, on the other hand, has influenced Manjusri, as Foucher had already pointed out. The same may also be said of Kartikeya.... The best-known Hindu deities are admitted wholesale into Buddhism, like Indra, Varuna, Maheshwara, Skanda, taken as keepers of the four quarters. Kama himself, the god of love, finds his place in the Buddhist Mandala. (Tucci, *Tibetan Painted Scrolls,* Vol. I, pp. 215-6.)

Not only this, all the complexities of Hindu ritualism, the *puja* with its eight or sixteen kinds of offerings, the libation *(homa),* the sacrificial fire lit with a special wood in pits purposely dug *(kunda),* were copied by the Buddhist tantrics. In fact Tibetan tantricism was very largely Saivite and Hindu.

Actually, at the time of the fifth Dalai Lama, a very large number of distinguished Indian scholars were residing and teaching in Lhasa. Of these, the most important were Gokula who had many disciples in the Tibetan capital, Krishnodaya of Banaras who translated Panini's *Dhatusutra,* and

Kshemagiri, a sanyasi of Mathura.

As at this time Tibet was the only point of contact between India and China, as both the north-western and the sea routes had been interrupted by other forces, this change in the character of Tibetan Buddhism was particularly important. It was Hindu Saivism in a Buddhist tantric garb that reached China from about the 13th century AD. The Mongols had improved the communications between Tibet and Peking and the influence of the Tibetan monks at the Mongol court, and generally in Mongolia, helped to spread the tantric ideas. The philosophical sects of Mahayana tended to weaken and in their place a curious mixture of Hinduism and Buddhism with tantric forms gained currency.

This influence on a much-reduced scale continued to the end of the Manchu regime. The Manchus kept up their spiritual relations with Lamaism, both in Mongolia and in Tibet, and therefore it may be said that even after the great period of Sino-Indian contacts which ended by about the 10th century, India and China continued to be connected via Tibet, though the cultural exchange was not of an important character.

Appendix II

Chinese Pilgrims in India

While no Indian traveller, monk or teacher has left us any record of China as he saw it, it is a matter of great significance that some of the Chinese pilgrims who visited India thought it necessary to enlighten their countrymen about conditions in India. This has indeed been a matter of some importance to us, as these records provide us with contemporary descriptions of social and political life in India. The historical tradition and geographical sense of the Chinese give these records a value far beyond their interest as depicting the condition of Buddhism in India at the time of their visits. A brief description of some of these records may help to give a fuller picture of Sino-Indian relationships.

Though the flow of pilgrims from China, at least from the 3rd to the 9th century AD, was continuous, we know the names of only a few of them. Thousands must have crossed the deserts or braved the dangers of the sea purely for acquiring merit by pilgrimages to the holy centres of Buddhism. But there were others whose object was not merely pilgrimage but also the improvement of their understanding of the great doctrines of the Buddha which they felt they understood only imperfectly through Chinese translations. The collection of sacred texts and relics was also considered a matter of importance. Education in India centres of learning, discussions with famous teachers, and direct inspiration from places hallowed by the Buddha's activity, these provided a powerful impetus to men of piety and scholarship to undertake the long and strenuous journey and spend years in a distant land.

Of the numerous pilgrims and students who visited India, the most notable of whom we have information are Fa Hien (399-414), Yuan Chuan* (Hiouen Tsang) (629-645), and I-tsing. Their names are better known in India than those of Kumarajiva, Bodhi Dharma, Paramartha and Vajrabodhi, scholars and saints who contributed much to the philosophical background in China. No doubt, all the three Chinese pilgrims were men of distinction, and Yuan Chuan was a scholar and saint who would have been honoured anywhere. He achieved a position of remarkable eminence in his own country; and in India, both at court and in learned circles, he was received as a great acharya. And yet, it is neither for his great piety nor for his saintliness that he is today remembered in India but almost wholly for the light that his 'Records' shed on the conditions of India in the first half of the 7th century.

Fa Hien, the earliest of these pilgrims, was a simple, believing soul who, unlike Yuan Chuan, was not particularly interested in what was happening around him. His work, known as the *Fo Kue Ki,* is therefore not of any great direct historical interest except as providing a picture of Buddhism in India at the end of the 4th century. It is characteristic of Fa Hien that though the period during which he travelled in India was the great age of Hindu revival under the Guptas, there is nothing in his work to indicate that, outside monasteries and other religious institutions of Buddhism, anything of significance existed in India.

Very little is known of the personality of Fa Hien. From 'The Memoirs of Eminent Monks' it is known that his family

---

* The original name of Yuan Chuan was Hiouen Tsang. Later, however, as one of the Emperors had a regnal name Hiouen, an edict was issued changing the monk's name of Yuan Chuan, which form I have used, following Watters. Both forms are correct.

name was Kung and that he was ordained at an early age. After that, all that we know is that he left for India in search of the complete copies of the *Vinaya Pitaka*. Fa Hien, with a companion, set out with the suite of an envoy and reached India after a dangerous and exciting journey.

Even more than his stay in India, it is his journey to and from India that is of great interest to us today. Leaving Chang An, Fa Hien took the outer route, crossing the Gobi Desert and going north, along the silk road. From a place which he calls Wooe, he struck south, skirting the high mountains, and reached Khotan. From there, the passage across the Hindukush to Uddiyana, the classic country of Mahayana Buddhism, was a well-frequented one as Khotan maintained the closest connection with the Kabul Valley. The first place of importance he visited in India proper was Mathura, which he describes as a great centre of Buddhism. From there he went on to Kanauj, Vaisali, Pataliputra, Kapilavastu and Banaras and seems to have been received hospitably everywhere. One comment he makes on conditions in India is particularly interesting. 'They have not', he says, 'to register their household or to attend to any magistrates and their rules.' In China, the Han dynasty had introduced the system of house census under which each household was supposed to report to the local magistrate. This must have been an oppressive procedure and Fa Hien's statement that in Madhya Desa they did not have to register their households sounds like a cry of relief.

At Jetavana, which was the first great monastery, hallowed by association with the Buddha himself, which he visited, Fa Hien felt a deep sense of fulfilment. The passage in which he describes the arrival at the monastery is touching.

> When Fa Hien and Tao Ching first arrived at Jetavana and thought how the World-honoured One had formerly resided there, painful reflections arose in their minds. Born in a borderland along with their like-minded friends, they had

> travelled through many kingdoms; some of those friends had returned [to China], some had [died], proving the impermanence and uncertainty of life; and today they saw the place where the Buddha had lived, now unoccupied by him.

Kapilavastu left him depressed for 'all was found in desolation'. But his greatest personal experience was the night he spent on the Vulture Peak, the Gridhrakuta, the sacred hill near Rajgriha, so dear to the Blessed One and so often frequented by him. There the pilgrim, desiring to evoke the Presence of the Master spent the night alone and returned the next morning with a feeling of beatitude.

Fa Hien spent three years in Pataliputra studying Sanskrit and copying the Vinaya texts. From there he proceeded to Tamralipti and embarked from there to Ceylon 'on a large merchant vessel'. After a peaceful journey of fourteen days, the pilgrim reached Ceylon where he undertook further studies for another two years. At the end of that period he embarked for Java en route for China. The journey to Java from Ceylon took ninety days. The route from Ceylon and the South Indian ports to China was a well-frequented one, in regular use by merchantmen going to the Far East. Although the journey took ninety days, the pilgrim had the satisfaction of knowing that he was now on his way back home after successfully completing a difficult mission.

The pious follower of Buddha found that in Java 'various forms of error and Brahminism were flourishing' and this caused him some pain. After spending some time there, he boarded another ship for China. Fa Hien spent altogether fifteen years in the holy task he had undertaken. He was moved by a faith which enabled him to overcome all difficulties and travel in strange and unfamiliar countries in search of knowledge and wisdom. His essentially human character comes out clearly in many parts of his book, the *Fo Kue Ki.* Especially moving is his description of the emotions that overtook him when, in Ceylon, he saw a worshipper, presumably a Chinese, making an offering of a Chinese fan at a temple. Fa Hien had been away so long, cut away from his people, his one companion Tao Ching having settled down in Gaya, hearing nothing from China, and not knowing when he would see his country again or whether he would be able to return at all, that at the mere sight of a Chinese fan nostalgia overtook him and tears flowed from his eyes. This little incident tells us more about the human qualities of Fa Hien than perhaps anything else in the book.

Yuan Chuan, our next pilgrim, is undoubtedly one of the most remarkable among men who have devoted themselves to the cause of a religion. In his lifetime he attained a position of unique eminence, being considered a friend and adviser by the Emperor, a Bodhisattva by his followers and a scholar and saint by everyone. After his death, his reputation has not dimmed. Even today, both in China and in India, his memory remains green, and the honour recently done to his name by the Chinese People's Republic, by giving to India a portion of his remains to be housed in a temple to be erected in Nalanda, is indicative of the respect paid to him by the peoples of both China and India.

Yuan Chuan came from a distinguished family of scholars who held office under the Empire. He was the youngest of his father's four sons. One of his elder brothers had become a monk and, following him, Yuan Chuan also was ordained at the age of twenty. The zeal, learning and eloquence of the young monk earned him fame in China, but the more he studied Buddhist scriptures in their Chinese translations, the more he was assailed by doubt about their exact meaning. A genuine searcher after truth, he was anxious to study the doctrines in the original language and to understand their true significance. This desire for knowledge, together with the ambition to visit the holy places sacred to his religion, led him to undertake the journey to India. There were many difficulties in the pilgrim's way. Imperial edicts prohibited anyone from leaving China without the permission of the Emperor. The way was long and arduous and, of course, Yuan Chuan, at that time, did not know Sanskrit. But to a young man of 29, animated by religious zeal, these difficulties seemed unimportant. He chose the northern route which, though long, was comparatively less difficult. Crossing the Gobi Desert, the pilgrim travelled as far west as Tashkand and from there turned to Samarkand, Balkh and Kabul, thus avoiding the Tienshan Mountains and the Pamir Plateau. The perils he had to face were many waterless deserts of unending sand, robbers, rivers in flood, dangerous mountain passes: yet his faith carried him through and he arrived in India in 630.

Yuan Chuan stayed in India for over fifteen years, travelling extensively all over the country. Although his interest was in religious studies, to which he devoted many years under celebrated teachers at the university of Nalanda, Yuan Chuan, in his travels, did not fail to observe the social and political conditions of the places he visited. In fact, we know more about India in the 7th century from his descriptions than from any other source, indigenous or foreign. The general description of India he gives is particularly interesting as may be seen from the passage quoted below:

> The towns and villages have inner gates; the walls are wide and high; the streets and lanes are tortuous, and the roads winding. The thoroughfares are dirty and the stalls arranged on both sides of the road with appropriate signs. Butchers, fishers, dancers, executioners, scavengers, and so on, have their abodes without the city. In coming and going these persons are bound to keep on the left side of the road till they arrive at their, homes. Their houses are surrounded by low walls, and form the suburbs. The earth being soft and muddy, the walls of the towns are mostly built of brick or tiles. The towers on the walls are constructed of wood or bamboo; the houses have

> balconies and belvederes, which are made of wood, with a coating of lime or mortar, and covered with tiles. The different buildings have the same form as those in China; rushes, or dry branches, or tiles, or boards are used for covering them. The walls are covered with lime or mud, mixed with cow's dung for purity. At different seasons they scatter flowers about. Such are some of their different customs. The *sangharamas* (monasteries) are constructed with extraordinary skill. A three-storeyed tower is erected at each of the four angles. The beams and the projecting heads are carved with great skill in different shapes. The doors, windows, and the low walls are painted profusely; the monks' cells are ornamental on the inside and plain on the outside. In the very middle of the building is the hall, high and wide. There are various storeyed chambers and turrets of different height and shape, without any fixed rule. The doors open towards the east; the royal throne also faces the east. Their clothing is not cut or fashioned; they mostly affect fresh white garments; they esteem little those of mixed colour or ornamented. The men wind their garments round their middle, then gather them under the armpits, and let them fall across the body, hanging to the right.

The social conditions of the time are also fully described by Yuan Chuan. After describing the castes in India, Yuan Chuan alludes to their habits.

> They mostly go barefooted; few wear sandals. They stain their teeth red or black. They bind their hair and pierce their ears. They are particular in their personal cleanliness. All wash before eating; they never use food left over from a former meal. Wooden and stone vessels must be destroyed after use. Metal ones must be well polished and rubbed. After eating, they cleanse their mouths with willow sticks and wash their hands and mouths.

To give further quotations would be unnecessary, but it may be noted that there is no aspect of Indian life that Yuan Chuan does not describe: social institutions, justice, administration, the character of the people, the system of taxation, etc. At the court of Harsha, where he spent some time, he was specially honoured and we have from him an interesting and valuable description at the Imperial Capital. But though an ardent Buddhist, Yuan Chuan was not prejudiced against the followers of Hinduism. His description of the Chalukya Kingdom and of the Maratha people are well worth quoting as showing the quality of his impartial observation.

> Ma-ho-la-ch'o [Maharashtra] is about 5,000 li [about 1,700 miles] in circuit. The capital borders on the west on a great river. It is about 30 li round. The soil is rich and fertile; it is regularly cultivated and very productive. The climate is hot; the disposition of the people is honest and simple; they are tall of stature and of a stern, vindictive character. To their benefactors they are grateful; to their enemies relentless. If they are insulted, they will risk their lives to avenge themselves. If they are asked to help one in distress, they will forget themselves in their haste to render assistance. If they are going to seek revenge, they first give their enemy warning; then, each being armed, they attack one another with lances. When one turns to flee, the other pursues him; but they do not kill a man who submits. If a general loses a battle, they do not inflict punishment, but present him with a woman's clothes, and so he is driven back to seek death for himself. The country provides for a band of champions to the number of several hundred. Each time they are about to engage in conflict then one man with lance in hand will meet ten thousand and challenge them to fight. If one of these champions meets a man and kills him, the laws of the country do not punish him. Every time they go forth, they beat drums before them. Moreover they inebriate many hundred head of elephants, and taking them out to fight, they themselves first drink their wine, and then, rushing forward in mass, they trample everything down, so that no enemy can stand before them. The king, in consequence of his possessing these men and elephants, treats his neighbours with contempt. He is one of the Kshatriya caste and his name is Pu-lo-ki-she [Pulikesi]. His plans and undertakings are widespread, and his beneficent actions are felt over a great distance. His subjects obey him with perfect submission.

Yuan Chuan spent five years at the university of Nalanda, where he studied the different systems of Indian philosophy with great care. His description of life in Nalanda is especially interesting. 'Learning and discussing they found the day too short. Day and night they admonished each other, juniors and seniors mutually helping to perfection.' His work at the university was so well appreciated that, when the rectorship fell vacant, the monks of the university offered him the post. But Yuan Chuan was pining to go back. Work awaited him there.

Yuan Chuan travelled most extensively in India, in the east up to Kamrup and Assam and in the south at least up to Kanchi [Kanchipuram]. It is doubtful whether he visited Ceylon, but he gives a description of it, perhaps on the basis of information from Buddhist monks he met at Kanchi. He travelled in Kalinga, Mahakosal, Andhra, Maharashtra and of course in the extensive dominions of Emperor Harsha. Describing Banaras, he says:

> The city wards were close together and the inhabitants were very numerous and had boundless wealth, their houses being full of rare valuables. The people were gentle and courteous and esteemed devotion to learning. The majority of them believed in the other systems and only a few of them were Buddhists.... of Deva temples there were over a hundred. The followers of Siva were persevering in austerities seeking release from mortal existence. In one of the temples, Yuan Chuan says, there was a "bell-metal image of the Deva, nearly a hundred feet high, which was life-like in its awe-inspiring majesty."

So, after a fifteen-year stay, the pilgrim made his preparations for the journey back to China. The manner of his return was totally different. He was escorted to the frontier of the Empire with great ceremony. The pilgrim carried with him 657 manuscripts, 50 relics of the Buddha, numerous images in gold, silver, crystal and sandalwood and a large collection of paintings. His arrival in Chang An was also in the nature of a triumph. He had left the capital secretly, in defiance of the Emperor's orders. But on hearing the news of his approach, the Son of Heaven with his whole court went outside the city gate to welcome him with honours such as had never been given to a subject before.

Yuan Chuan's life in China is not of relevance to us in this discussion, but it may be noted that the prestige he had acquired was so great that the Emperor had a nine storeyed Tower of Victory erected for him and he was provided with the necessary facilities to undertake the great work of translation. The rest of his life Yuan Chuan devoted to this great work and also, at the request of the Emperor, to composing a record of his observations, which has since then been accepted as one of the great classics of travel literature. In his introduction Yuan Chuan says:

> I have set forth at length the natural scenery and ascertained territorial divisions. I have explained the qualities of national customs and climatic characteristics. Moral conduct is not constant and tasks vary. When matters can not be thoroughly investigated, one may not be dogmatic. Wherever I went, I made notes and, in maintaining what I saw and heard, I recorded the aspirations of civilization.

In appearance, Yuan Chuan was tall and handsome, with penetrating eyes and a prominent forehead. His manners were dignified and courtly and the impression he made on the great men of the day may be judged from the honour paid to him by Harsha, by the Tang emperor, and by the abbots and monks of Nalanda. Harsha went to the extent of issuing a proclamation that 'if anyone should hurt or touch the pilgrim, he should at once be beheaded and whoever spoke against him should have his tongue cut out'. We have already alluded to the pre-eminence he was able to attain among the scholars of Nalanda.

Even after his return to China he did not forget his friends and fellow students of Nalanda. Some of Yuan Chuan's letters in Sanskrit to his friends in Nalanda have recently been discovered and published.

Two inexplicable omissions in the *Si Yu Ki,* Yuan Chuan's Record of Travels, may be noticed. Though the pilgrim spent a considerable time in Andhra country he makes no allusions to Amaravati Tope, the great centre at an earlier time of Buddhist learning in that part of India. Nor does he allude to Sanchi with its great Stupa and monasteries situated in the heart of Harsha's own dominions. Sanchi must have been a place of exceptional importance to the Buddhists in the 7th century, and yet there is no allusion to it. Again, though Yuan Chuan visited the Chalukya capital of Vatapi and gives a fine description of Maharashtra country, he seems to be unaware of the existence of Ajanta, which must have been at the height of its glory at that time. These are problems for which no explanation is available.

I-tsing, the third Chinese pilgrim we shall deal with, was a junior contemporary of Yuan Chuan. His interest, apart from performing the pilgrimage, was in reforming the *Vinaya* or the discipline of the monasteries. Born in 635, I-tsing joined the Order at an early age and achieved distinction as a scholar-monk. At the age of 35, when he was in Chang An, the capital, the call came to him to make the pilgrimage. This is how he describes it:

> At the time, there were with me Chuyi, teacher of the Law of Ping Pu; Hung-i, teacher of the Sastra of Lai Chow; and also two or three other *bhadantas*. We all made an agreement together to visit the Vulture Peak (Gridhra Kuta) and set our hearts on seeing the Bhodi tree. Chuyi was, however, drawn by his affection towards his home in Ping Chuan, for his mother was of an advanced age, whereas Hung-i turned his thoughts to Sukhavati on meeting Hiuen Chan in Kiangning. Hieun Khei [one of the party] came as far as Kwangtung. He, however, like others, changed his mind, which he had formerly made up. So I had to start for India only with a young priest, Shan-huey of Tsin Chou.

I-tsing travelled to India by the sea route. Boarding one of the regular boats sailing to the southern islands, he reached Sri Vijaya, the capital of the great empire which covered both Sumatra and the Peninsula of Malaya. Sri Vijaya, at this time, was a great centre of Indian culture, and an ideal place for one coming from China to prepare himself by the study of languages for a stay in India. I-tsing began to learn Sanskrit there and, in time, took another ship which brought him to the great port of Tamralipti in Bengal. On the way to Tamralipti, the boat touched the Nicobar Islands whose naked and primitive inhabitants excited his interest.

On arrival at Tamralipti, I-tsing met a disciple of Yuan Chuan with whom he began to study Sanskrit grammar. After thoroughly preparing himself in this manner the monk, along with a few other pilgrims, joined a party of merchants going to Nalanda. The adventures that befell them on this journey are thus described by I-tsing:

> At a distance of ten days from Mahabodhi Vihara, we passed a great mountain and bogs. The pass is dangerous and difficult to cross. It is important to proceed in a company of several men and never to proceed alone. All that time I, I-tsing, was attacked by an illness of the season. My body was fatigued and without strength. I sought to follow the company of merchants but, tarrying and suffering as I was, I was unable to reach them. I alone remained behind and walked in the dangerous defiles without a companion. Late in the day, when the sun was about to set, some mountain brigands made their appearance. Drawing a bow and shouting aloud, they came and glared at me and one after another insulted me. First they stripped me of my upper robe and then took off my undergarment.

Then a fearful thought came to the monk's mind. He had heard rumours of the habits of the hill tribes of sacrificing fair-coloured people to the *devi*. The worship of Vindhya Nivasini, with its horrifying rites of sacrifice, was indeed not uncommon during this period among the primitive tribes of the Vindhya Hills. I-tsing was a fair young man of 37, in every way a suitable person to be sacrificed to the dread goddess. It is not surprising that the monk got freshened. An idea struck him. 'Thereupon', he says, 'I entered a muddy hole, and besmeared all my body with mud. I covered myself with leaves and supporting myself on a stick I advanced slowly.' He must indeed have looked a strange figure, covered with mud and clothed in leaves, but this disguise saved him. Without any further trouble he caught up with the party the same night.

Of I-tsing's journeys in India, we know very little. He must have done the usual pilgrimages, Rajgirh, to see the Vulture Peak, Bodh Gaya, to see the Bodhi Tree, to Lumbini Gardens to worship at the place of the Master's nativity, and to Banaras, where the Enlightened One preached his first sermon. After this, he settled down at Nalanda for ten years to make an exhaustive study of the *Vinaya* texts.

I-tsing's report is a very short document, more in the nature of an introduction to his detailed and comprehensive work on Vinaya, or the disciplinary procedures of monasteries. This is a work of exceptional value as it describes the social habits of Indians at that time. There are chapters on the wearing of garments, on habits of personal cleanliness, on sleeping and resting, on proper conduct, on the relations between teachers and pupils, in fact on every aspect of human behaviour. This is what I-tsing says about after-meal cleanliness:

> When a meal is finished, do not fail to cleanse the hands. In getting the water, fetch a water jar for yourself or order others to do so. Chew tooth wood in the mouth. Let the tongue as well as the teeth be carefully cleansed.

He gives detailed instructions on how water should be strained:

> The Indians use fine white cloth for straining water and in

> China fine silk should be used after having slightly boiled it with rice cream, etc.

If I-tsing's book gives us limited knowledge of geography or political conditions, it provides us with invaluable material about the social habits of Indians in the 7th century. From that point of view, it is a work of unique importance.

After I-tsing's time also, large numbers of pilgrims continued to visit India. But no record of their activities has come down to us.

Appendix III

The Interactions of India and China on Art

The influence of India on the painting, sculpture and architecture of China forms a most interesting subject of study. Equally the influence of Chinese painting on certain aspects of Mughal miniature painting and of Chinese architecture in the domestic architecture of the hill areas of North India are matters which no one interested in the impact of culture could neglect. So far, however, there has been no comprehensive study of this subject and, except for scrappy essays and allusions in general works on Chinese art, there is very little published material available.

The earliest traceable influence of India in Chinese art is in the Yun Kang Caves. These caves were excavated from AD 460 onwards for a period of forty years. The sculptures in these caves are mainly Buddhist although in Caves VII, VIII and X there are many images of Hindu divinities. In the gateway of Cave VIII are two images, one of Siva on his Nandi and another of Vishnu on Garuda. But the main images are of the Buddha, or of bodhisattvas or relate to stories in the Jatakas. Regarding the Buddha images, the two Japanese scholars who have jointly published in fifteen volumes a truly magnificent study of these cave temples say: 'A search for their Indian prototype leads one not so much to the mature Gupta style as seen in the seated Sarnath image... as to the Maṭhura school of the earlier Gupta period.' Again, the same authors point out that in the five caves of Tan Yao and in the central caves almost 'all the Buddha heads are without trace of hair represented'. In the Gandhara sculptures, wavy hair is a significant feature.

Apart, of course, from the fact that the ideals and the stories represented in the images and friends came from India and therefore, they reflected at all times in a measure the culture and thought of India, it is also a recognized fact that images that came from India were considered specially holy. Omura, in his *History of Chinese Sculpture*, has collected literary references which clearly establish this point. There is no doubt, as Sickman and Soper emphasize in their recent work, *Art And Architecture of China*, that the style followed in the 4th and 5th centuries were ultimately derived from Gandharan and Indian models. This is especially true of the art in the Yun Kang Caves. In the Sui period that followed we have other cave temples. The earlier sculptures in these caves also show a dominant Indian influence. Indeed Sickman and Soper go so far as to say that

> the sculpture of the classic Gupta period of India (AD 320-600) was the most powerful and direct stimulus to Chinese sculpture in the second half of the 6th century'. 'However', they add, 'it is much easier to speak loosely of strong Indian influence than to illustrate the argument with clear comparisons. Although, in many instances, the Indian devotion to solid plastic form in the human body and India's love of luxuriant plant growth are reflected in the work of Chinese sculptors, these elements, at times vaguely understood, have become so characteristically Chinese that it is seldom possible to point to any specific Indian parent example or school (*Art and Architecture of China*, p. 53).

At a place called Hsiang Tan Shan there is a series of cave temples, the sculpture of which shows clear influence of the Gupta style. The representation of jewellery, finely executed with details, are in the Indian style. It is also stated that

> the lotus leaves and thick vine stems of the designs have also

> strong affinities with the sub-tropical verdure in Indian sculpture from as early as the Stupa of Sanchi (c. 75-25 BC) to the sculptures of the Mathura School and the Ajanta cave temples of the Gupta times.

Belonging to this period is also the famous image of Avilokiteswara, now in the Boston Museum. It is claimed that

> its affinities with Indian concepts are evident in the fleshy and sensuous modelling of hands, feet and face, as well as in the profusion of jewellery. The déhanche pose so beloved by the sculptors of India is very timidly essayed.

In the southern and south-eastern areas of China, which came under Tantric influence from Tibet, Indian sculpture, especially images of Tantric deities, continued to be popular. These influences could not, however, be said to have affected the artistic tradition of China or contributed to its richness. They merely satisfied a provincial taste.

So far as painting is concerned, the first great centre of Indian influence is Tunghuan.* It is indeed a cave city, in which every chapel hollowed out of the hill is covered with mural paintings. The sculpture in Tunghuan is not particularly interesting as the material of the cliff was unsuitable for it. It is the wonderful series of mural paintings that makes Tunghuan a veritable treasure-house of Sino-Indian art.

The very idea of mural paintings in cave temples came from India where it was a well-established tradition from at least the 2nd century BC. With the excavation of Ajanta in the 2nd century of the Christian era, mural paintings in caves seem to have become popular with Buddhists. Through Central Asia this tradition reached China, taking on in its process many special characteristics of Central Asian Art. But its basic

* For a fuller description of Tunghuan, see the author's work, *In Two Chinas*.

Indian inspiration is something which is obvious. While many of the figures are formalized, the more individual paintings of single figures often show distinct Indian characteristics.

The Tunghuan paintings were, no doubt, only provincial art, but it is interesting to note the continuous introduction of Indian themes and motives at different times. With the Tibetan occupation of the Tunghuan area after the 10th century, we have the first Tantric paintings of a distinctly Indian character. The Tantric deities make their appearance alongside Hindu gods like Ganesha. Also, so far as Tunghuan is concerned, it is interesting to note that in the cave paintings one can see the entire system of Indian *mudras* or expressive gestures which had been evolved as a language for representation from very early times. In fact, many of the symbolisms and motifs of Indian religious art came to be incorporated in the art of Buddhism everywhere—the bodhi tree, the nimbus, the yakshas who guard the temples, etc. For over a period of seven hundred years, the cave city was a centre of great artistic activity in which the Indian, Persian, Central Asian and Chinese traditions freely mingled. No doubt, in the end, the genius of China asserted itself within its own cultural areas, but the Indian themes and symbols continued to the very end. In that sense, Tunghuan paintings represent a continuous synthesis of Indian and Chinese ideas. Though its influence was localized, being situated in a distant frontier area, in the middle of a desert, though its character was never higher than that of a distinctive provincial art, Tunghuan is still of the highest importance in art history, no less by the length of its creative period as by the continuous admixture of India, Chinese and Central Asian traditions in painting.

Of the temple painters of the Tang period, the most famous was Wu Tao-tzu. Though no work of his has come down to us, we know that his great masterpiece was entitled,

'The Subjugation of Mara', a theme of unfailing interest to Buddhists.

A remarkable school of painting directly connected with Indian thought, though not with Indian artistic tradition, became popular in the 12th and 13th centuries. The Dhyana school (Chan in Chinese) of which Bodhi Dharma, who arrived in Nanking in AD 520, was the founder has already been briefly described in the second lecture. His main teaching was that the Buddha nature in oneself was the only reality. 'The Absolute is immanent in everyone's heart', he declared. Discover the unreality of the world by meditation and thus realize the truth, was his teaching. This conception of a reality, a form of the Indian doctrine of maya, influenced every aspect of the life of this school. Though the sect got divided into a northern and southern school and the northern became associated with pomp and outward show, both influenced the art of painting. The experience of realization, known to Indian thought as Brahmananda, is a stage which the Chan masters describe as one in which it becomes impossible to differentiate knowledge and truth and in which man is in a state of indescribable ecstasy. Clearly, such a state cannot be described by words but the experience can be suggested by paintings 'which may bring the prepared observer nearer to the awareness of his own enlightenment'. Also the oneness of nature with man was a doctrine of the Chan School which led to their cultivation of nature. Consequently, the school of painting which Chan Buddhism developed had a closer approach to nature. According to learned authorities,

> Terseness and brevity, clarifying mental vision and intensity of realization are all prerequisites of the Chan painter. The monochrome ink technique in which the pliant brush can move with the rapidity of thought was ideally suited to the expressionist paintings of the Chan School.

For the Chan painters, it is said,

> the extremely rapid and always abbreviated recording of the subjects from nature in a few pools of wash or staccato brush strokes made for a transference to painting of the instantaneous and intuitive perception of the oneness in the workings of nature that dominated Chan Buddhist thought.

This school of early expressionism covered a very wide range of subjects. Basically, however, they fall into two classes, studies of nature and portraits of Chan masters. The portrait of Bodhi Dharma, a favourite subject of Chan painters, was itself a masterly achievement. Helen B. Chapin has published a study entitled 'Three Early Portraits of Bodhi Dharma' in the *Archives of the Chinese Art Society of America* which show that the Chan painters had evolved an ideal portrait of the Patriarch in keeping with his doctrine.

The greatest master of the Chan School was Mu'chi, whose work, now preserved mainly in Japan, shows Chan painting at its best. A priest-artist who revolted against the formalism of the Yuan period, Mu'chi brought to his art a freshness and realism born of a contempt of the world, which gave to his realism great power and imagination. One of his most famous paintings is of a mother ape on a tree clutching its young. This is said to be a satire on Confucius whose emphasis was, of course, on family life. Another painting of his, which brings out even more clearly the Indian influence on him, is entitled, 'The Chan Master in Meditation', which shows an immense serpent curling around a holy man in meditation and raising its angry head. This, of course, is a common enough conception in India, but in China it is specially characteristic of the Chan or Dhyana School.

Another great master who deserves mention is Liang Ki, a court painter brought up in the classical tradition who was awarded the highest honour by the State. But later in life, he became interested in Chan Buddhism and began to paint in the expressionist style peculiar to that school. His famous picture, 'The Sixth Patriarch Tearing Up the Sutras', is characteristic of the Chan school of painting. It is meant to illustrate the Chan view that to know all the scriptures does not mean realization. The following description of the technique of this masterpiece will serve to underline what Chan painting stood for:

> Every brush stroke in the painting is brittle and explosive. The simple composition in its expressive angularity is as carefully constructed as the work of the old masters.

After the 13th century, Indian influence in painting also waned, mainly as a result of the stagnation in Buddhist life. Images of the Buddha continued to be made in the traditional manner and paintings of Buddhist themes were also popular in monasteries; but Buddhist art ceased to have life when Buddhism, itself ceased to grow, deprived of its contacts with India.

In the field of architecture, India's contribution was not as notable as that in either painting or sculpture. But in the temple architecture of Buddhism, Indian influences could be seen from the beginning.

The Chinese pagoda architecture was modelled mainly on the great structures erected by Buddhist monarchs in north-west India. These great pagodas, especially the one near modern Peshawar, which was built in the 2nd century AD, were many storeyed buildings, and were impressive in their massiveness and beauty. The pilgrim, Sung Yun, who saw it in the 6th century, after it had been destroyed and restored many times, describes the tower as having thirteen storeys, with thirteen gold discs at the top. The total height was said to be 700 wei feet. This building seems to have provided the model for the many-storeyed pagodas of the Chinese Buddhists. Examples of other Indian styles also are not unusual. On Mount Sung in Honan is a pagoda which is claimed

> to be an exceptionally faithful reproduction of some Indian

> model of contemporary Gupta style. The plan is a dodecagon of brick. There is a high plain plinth, and then a *piano nobile* with corner columns. The remainder is a succession of corbelled eaves, diminishing along as elegant curve and topped by a masonry replica of the usual marks and disks. Details are purely Indian. (Sickman and Soper, *Art and Architecture of China*, p. 230.)

The traditional Indian style of stupa was not popular in China; but in Shantung there are temples which approximate to the Indian stupa style. The famous Asoka reliquary temple is described in Chinese books as being like stupas. Also, near the famous Wu-tai Shan temple are the remains of an old pagoda whose

> original prototype was unquestionably Indian, the kind of stupa found in the Gupta caves at Ajanta. It seems to have been carried to China as a part of the baggage of the most fashionable tantric sect: a similar form was part of the architectural repertory of the Tunghuan painters from the mid-century.

In the Liao period (10th century), there is further evidence of Indian influence in temple architecture, mainly as a result of the growing influence of Tantric Buddhism. In the Liao temples, the ground plan is generally octagonal, based on the Indian Tantric conception of the eight quarters (the *Astadik*) which is also the cosmological pattern of the Tantrics.

Of one major effort to copy a purely Indian style of construction we have direct evidence. The Ming Annals record that in the reign of Yung Lo, in 1404, some Indian pandits visited his court and presented him with five images of the Buddha and a detailed plan of the Bodh Gaya temple. The Emperor ordered the construction of five temples, replicas on a smaller scale of the Gaya temple and these can still be seen just outside Peking. They represent Indian architecture in its purest tradition.

It is difficult to estimate Chinese influence in Indian

artistic traditions. The gabled roofs of houses on the west coast of India show a marked Chinese influence. When and how this style reached Kerala we do not know, but the similarity is too marked to be put down to an independent evolution in this part of India. Again, in the hill areas of the Himalayan region both temple and domestic architecture show Chinese influences which no doubt penetrated through Tibet. The Buddhist temples in Nepal are more of the pagoda than of the stupa style; the outer ornamentations also show Chinese influence.

In painting, the specifically Indian tradition does not seem ever to have been influenced by China, but the Mughal paintings undoubtedly show Chinese influences, especially in the treatment of clouds and rocks. This influence reached India not directly from China but through Iran which, from the time of the II Khans, seems to have borrowed to some extent from Chinese artistic traditions. In any case, the earlier Mughal miniatures undoubtedly have traces of Chinese influence.

It has also been suggested that Indian jade carving, which became popular only from the time of the Mughals, might have been influenced by the Chinese. This is likely, though the evidence in favour of this belief is meagre. It is true that no particular value was attached to jade in India and the fashion in this connection might well have come from China through the Mughals.

On the whole, it may be said on present evidence that the influence of China on the artistic development of India has been negligible.